Studies in the
Classical Theories
of Money

AMS PRESS
NEW YORK

Studies in the
Classical Theories
of Money

KARL H. NIEBYL

COLUMBIA UNIVERSITY PRESS

New York · 1946

Library of Congress Cataloging in Publication Data

Niebyl, Karl Heinrich, 1906–
    Studies in the classical theories of money.

    Bibliography: p.
    1. Money.   2. Inflation (Finance)   I. Title.
II. Title: Classical theories of money.
HG221.N65 1973   332.4'01   70-173795
ISBN 0-404-04709-2

From the edition of 1946, New York
First AMS edition published in 1973
Manufactured in the United States of America

AMS PRESS INC.
NEW YORK, N.Y. 10003

PARENTIBUS
FILIUS
GRATUS

IT IS . . . WORTHY OF OBSERVATION THAT so deep-rooted is the prejudice which considers coin and bullion as things essentially differing in all their operations from other commodities, that writers greatly enlightened upon the general truth of political economy seldom fail, after having requested their readers to consider money and bullion merely as commodities subject to "the same general principles of supply and demand which are unquestionably the foundation on which the whole superstructure of political economy is built"; to forget this recommendation themselves, and to argue upon the subject of money, and the laws which regulate its export and import, as quite distinct and different from those which regulate the export and import of other commodities.—DAVID RICARDO: Appendix to *The High Price of Bullion, a Proof of the Depreciation of Bank Notes.*

THE ONLY VERY IMPORTANT THING to be said about currency is that it is not nearly as important as it looks.—ALFRED MARSHALL, in a letter to James Bonar.

Preface

THESE STUDIES were written before the present emergency, as parts of an inquiry into basic concepts of monetary theory. A definite need was felt for an investigation into the formation of doctrines, in order to return monetary analysis from its present function as a guide book to economic post mortems, to a tool in the formulation of policy.

In 1940 and 1941 the author acted as an advisor on monetary and fiscal policies to the Consumer Commissioner of the National Defense Commission. It was at that time that traditionalist economists and a vociferous part of the public began to raise the cry about the threat of a runaway inflation, and with —*post hoc, propter hoc*—songs about the "inflationary gap," with their contrapuntal intricacies, tried to persuade the general public to look backwards and get scared rather than look forward and deal adequately with a newly developing economic reality.

Because of these theoretical preconceptions representing straight-line projections of misconceived past experiences into the present and the future, it was realized once more that only a historical and material analysis of monetary theoretical thinking could help to dispel the veil that "received doctrine" was spreading over current events. On the basis of such an analysis—the major historical part of which is presented here in the following studies—the author argued and still argues that the concept of inflation has a historical content subject to qualitative change, the understanding of which invalidates for the conditions of the present most, if not all, the judgments traditionally implied in it.

Inadequate theories lead to inadequate policies, and inadequate policies are "inadequate" for the interest and the welfare of society as a whole, while at the same time they are "adequate"—over the short run—for vested and functionally past economic interests. The need to re-examine our analytical tools is strongly indicated, for instance, by the continued unequal distribution of the burden of financing social expenditures, as well as by the endowment of the Little Steel Formula with rather mystical powers to avoid a nonimminent inflation. At the same time, the use of the formula effects a decrease in real income by freezing a discrepancy between wages and a controlled increase in prices which is unjustified either by the developments in the civilian sector of the economy or by the actual use made of the purchasing power in the hands of the people. The expropriationary implications of Keynesian war finance methods, in the once-again-revived *Depositenlegende,* which aims to prevent federal social initiative in the re-employment of otherwise, shall we say, technologically deployed monetary resources, are other examples.

The method employed in these Studies is by no means new. It has grown and developed since the last half of the nineteenth century. The manner in which the author has used this *qualitatively changing* methodology of scientific economic analysis has been discussed elsewhere.[1] It may prove helpful in the final evaluation of the historical analysis presented here and its significance for the present to have recourse to that exposition.

The author is indebted to the editor of the *American Economic Review* for permission to make use of an earlier article of his "A Re-examination of the Classical Theory of Inflation," published in the issue of December, 1940, XXX, 759–773. The following publishers kindly gave me permission to quote from the books listed below: Prentice-Hall, Inc., *Predecessors of Adam Smith,* by E. A. J. Johnson, and *The Theory of Prices,* by Arthur W. Marget; Harper & Brothers, *Studies in the*

---

[1] Niebyl, "The Need for a Concept of Value in Economic Theory," *Harvard Quarterly Journal of Economics* LIV (February, 1940), 201–216.

Theory of International Trade, by Jacob Viner; Harvard University Press, *Early Economic Thought,* by A. E. Monroe; Longmans, Green and Co., *Principles of Political Economy,* by John Stuart Mill, and *Tudor Economic Documents,* by R. H. Tawney; The Macmillan Co., *The Mathematical Principles of the Theory of Wealth,* by August Cournot; and the Oxford University Press, *The Westminster Bank through a Century* and *Select Statutes, Documents and Reports Relating to British Banking,* by T. E. Gregory.

Among the many colleagues and friends who read parts or the whole of the manuscript in its various stages, special acknowledgment is due to Professors James Angell of Columbia University, Erich Roll of the University of Hull, England, Frank Fetter of Haverford College, Clarence E. Bonnett of Tulane University, Dr. Joseph E. Reeve of the Bureau of the Budget and Professor Arthur Rowland Burnstan of Carleton College. To R. G. Hawtrey, Esq., Assistant Secretary of HM's Treasury, London; Dr. Pere Jacobson, Director of the Bank of International Settlements at Basle, Switzerland; to various members of the staff of the Economics Section of the League of Nations, Geneva, as well as to Professor Friederich von Hayek of the London School of Economics, I am grateful for the discussion of points of controversy which helped in the final formulation of my ideas. It is needless to say that none of them can be held responsible for any of the interpretations or conclusions expressed in the following pages.

Beyond the means of formal recognition is the debt which these Studies owe to my many friends and students. It was inside as well as outside the classroom; in the offices, halls and educational meetings of the trade unions; in government committees and in informal discussions that incentives were born and strenghtened to look at the problems facing us from new and perhaps more appropriate angles.

These Studies would never have seen the light of day if not for the labors of Miss Elizabeth Crosby Hale, who in my absence gave final shape to the manuscript and saw it completely through the press. Mrs. Frances Dodge checked the bibliographical references and helped with the final preparation of the manuscript. For work at earlier stages I am indebted to the painstaking secretarial labors of Miss Jeanne Ann Blodgett and Miss Marion Meiser.

Grants in aid of the research involved in this country and abroad were received from the Social Science Research Council, New York, and the Carleton College Research Fund, Carleton College, Northfield, Minnesota. Assistance was given by the Tulane University Research Fund to provide some secretarial help. These grants are gratefully acknowledged.

KARL H. NIEBYL

With the U.S. Naval forces in the Pacific
October, 1944

Contents

Part I · *The Function of Money in Early Industrial Society*

1 · Methodological Introduction

IT is the purpose of this study to furnish the tools for an understanding of the mechanics and dynamics of the flow of money. We wish to know why our monetary mechanism functions as it does.

It is a commonplace statement that social and economic phenomena as we observe them today have developed, or, as we say, have a history. Modern sociological and psychological investigations, as well as economic institutional research, have taught us that many of the explanations current today were constructed to a considerable extent to fit circumstances different from those to which their material content refers. One way of disentangling the mass of divergent, if not contradictory, statements concerning money is therefore to investigate the institutional development of the function of money.

History develops in phases, and these phases in turn are distinguished by certain basic characteristics. Therefore we have grown accustomed to making divisions in economic history—for instance, differentiating between feudal institutions and those of industrial capitalism. The historical phase of which our present-day monetary institutions form a part is industrial society.

Each phase of social history presents its own characteristic development. Although the early changes in a new period are still overshadowed by the institutions of the preceding period, there comes a time within this development when the young institutions have grown strong enough to be little influenced by those of the past. Within such a period of relatively unhampered expansion we can observe most clearly the basic institutions of that specific mode of production. They are no longer struggling against survival values, nor are they as yet forced to take on warped forms because of difficulties and rigidities which develop organically in later phases of their life span.

As far as our own economic institutions are concerned, this period falls into the last part of the eighteenth and the first part of the nineteenth centuries, and it is in order to show in their *highest degree of clarity* and *their lowest degree of complexity* our present-day economic institutions with special reference to the function of money that we have chosen this period for the starting point of our analysis.

Economic thought or theory constitutes that human activity by means of which the active members of the economic process attempt to cope with the particular problems presented to them at that time. It has been a common fallacy among economists since J. B. Say to believe that economic doctrines develop *in vacuo*. Recently some economists have tended towards the conclusion that economic doctrines, in order to carry meaning, must be related to the particular problem of the time in which they are created. John Maynard Keynes's formulation of this point has already become classic: "The postulates of the classical theory are applicable to a special case only . . . the characteristics of the special case assumed by the classical theory happen not to be those of the economic society in which we actually live." [1]

This state of affairs does not mean, however, that there is no value in the teaching of received doctrine, and by "received doctrine" we mean that which has been handed down from an earlier economic period. Quite the contrary is true. If we study received doctrine in the way proposed above, that is, as an attempt to cope with the concrete, contemporary economic circumstances, we shall be able to attain an invaluable insight into the necessary technique of coping with our own concrete problems. Secondly, however, and even more important, is that an adequate understanding of our modern institutions presupposes a satisfactory knowledge of the historical

[1] Keynes, *The General Theory of Employment, Interest, and Money*, p. 3.

development of these institutions. The continuity of received doctrine, therefore, is not safeguarded in the way in which some of the economists of the past have tried to safeguard it, that is, by removing and separating the doctrine from economic reality; but it may be safeguarded by *carefully anchoring it in the continuity of reality.*

With this general approach in mind we shall now attempt to present the historical background, that is to say, the early stage in the development of our modern institutions. It is not our purpose to write a minute and complete history of economics. We are going to stress only the changing function of money within the general background of developing industrial society.

2 · The Developing Necessity for a Monetary Standard

THE PRODUCTION AND EXCHANGE OF INDUSTRIAL COMMODITIES The latter part of the eighteenth century has generally been called the age of the Industrial Revolution. In the process of the emancipation of labor, guilds for the protection of handicraft were the first form of free labor production. The growth of production and the broadening of the markets necessitated an increasingly large application of capital. The latter was provided by the merchants, who, by means of the "putting-out" system, developed into industrial entrepreneurs, that is, producers. The need for greater efficiency in production induced the transfer of the actual productive activity from the homes of the workers into specially erected plants where industrial co-operation was possible. This period, commonly called the "period of manufacture," is the real cradle of the industrial mode of production.

Up to that time money functioned predominantly as a means for facilitating the exchange of finished products. Even in the "putting-out" system, the main interest of the capital investor was the same as that of the merchant: the sale of the finished goods. If we investigate the ideas about money current at that time, we shall find that in the minds of the political economists the only problems seem to have been the obtaining of an adequate supply of money for the purpose of exchanging commodities and the insurance of a relative stability of that money by inducing the authorities—in this period, the monarchs—to abstain from debasing the currency. As implied, the medium of exchange was exclusively precious metals.

At the moment when manufacturing enterprise came into existence, an entirely new aspect of money began to develop. The small entrepreneur was now emancipating himself from the trade function. He produced and made his profits by producing, leaving the servicing of the market to the merchant.

The result was that a medium had to be created for transferring the profits made in trade to the entrepreneur for the purpose of investment.[1] This was the more necessary since competition forced the small-scale entrepreneur to expand,[2] and the rate of expansion was far outdistancing the profits of production available for reinvestment. At the same time, the merchant was interested in an increased volume of output as well as in a place to invest his profits.

If we want to make, at this stage, a first attempt to define the function of money, we can say that the function of money depends upon the character and the relations of the particular factors of the economic process for which it serves as an interconnecting link. We propose to understand money always by what it does, never by abstractions which on the surface seem to be similar for different periods. It should already be clear at this early stage of our inquiry that there is little connection between the function of money in mercantile society and the role of money under the conditions of industrial production.

This point will prove to be of importance, since we shall see that in the development of industrial institutions the concrete relations of the productive process seem to recede increasingly into the background and therewith into the subconscious of the economically acting individual. However, since to the small-scale entrepreneur of the outgoing eighteenth century money was simply a means of payment for the factors which he needed for production, we do not need to be concerned as yet with the fetish character of money. Money was at that time a means to an end and had not yet appeared as an end in itself.

[1] Approximate amount of capital necessary for the setting up of enterprises is given in *Description of All Trades,* anonymous. For Birmingham hardware, £500 to £2,000 (*ibid.,* p. 18); for fire-engine makers, £500 (*ibid.,* p. 172); for potters, £1,000 (*ibid.,* p. 173).

[2] The difficulties in the securing of capital could not be overcome at that stage of the development by creating joint-stock companies. Adam Smith saw correctly that the "only trades which it seems possible for a joint-stock company to carry on successfully . . . are those of which all the operations are capable of being reduced to what is called a routine" (Adam Smith, *The Wealth of Nations,* II, 246), and in the enumeration of such trades Smith implies that ordinary manufacture had not even at his time advanced to this stage.

THE NECESSITY FOR A MONETARY STANDARD   As a direct reflection of the changes in the productive process, we observe during this period a change in the character of the markets in which the commodities produced were being sold. Though the character of the commodities sold in the form of consumers' goods did not seem to have changed very much, the consumers themselves had changed radically. Mercantile exchange was relatively simple in its dealings, which were predominantly with large individual consumers, merchants in other countries, the courts, the army, the cities. Such unimportant retail trade as then existed was also covered entirely by these merchant houses. These conditions were changed completely by the creation of the industrial laborer as consumer. The large masses of people in the preceding period had partaken of trade only to the extent of purchasing the absolute necessities of life: salt, spices, simple tools, and so forth, the bulk of their consumptive needs being satisfied by the products of their own agricultural or semi-agricultural activities. The transplantation of the worker from the "putting-out" system in his own home to work in factories in the cities and the consequent tremendous growth of the cities created an entirely new type of consumer demand, which in its relative complexity made new demands upon the type of money which was needed to accomplish this increasingly complicated distributive mechanism.

In the dealings between large merchants, precious metals could easily be weighed. While the demand for relative stability of currency, that is, coins of stable weight, had been voiced already in the preceding period, changes in the weight of coins and therewith in the value of the medium of exchange tended to bring about much more devastating consequences in the new type of market.

The result of this development was the gradual formulation of a demand for a generally acceptable standard of value. All participants in the productive process, including its guardian, the government, had to be made to adhere to this fixed value under threats of mutual reprisal.

BIMETALLISM We have indicated above that any medium of exchange can be explained only in reference to its proper historical and functional setting. From the time of the revival of trade to the nineteenth century, both gold and silver were used as media of exchange. It must be stated emphatically that this fact alone does not constitute the conditions for a bimetallic standard, "as a bimetallic standard needs for its efficient working certain definite conditions. It is a system in which the movement in or out of the country of an appreciable quantity of either metal can affect the value of the monetary unit, and in which, when one metal moves out, the other automatically moves in. The unit of currency must be exchangeable for both metals and both metals must be exchangeable for the currency, at fixed rates and in unlimited quantities." [3] As these conditions did not exist to sufficient extent up to the end of the eighteenth century it would be fallacious to speak of a "bimetallic standard" during the period of prevailing trade capitalism. Only after the development of small-scale industry with its resulting creation of a home market demand represented by wage laborers as well as with the increasing need for capital goods, do we observe conditions of sufficient integration for a generally valid standard of value to be at all possible. It will be our objective now to outline more specifically these conditions.

Fundamental to the working of a monetary standard is the possibility of an automatically working production mechanism. This mechanism was gradually provided by a developing free competitive economic system in which the growth of the small-scale entrepreneur and of the home demand offered such a basis. The close interdependence between producers and consumers insured that any changes in the value of the media of exchange would be communicated immediately to the whole market, and by "market" we mean by this time national markets rather than local markets.

With the growth of national industry in England, the rela-

[3] Feavearyear, *The Pound Sterling*, p. 19.

tions with other nations (especially Holland, but also with France and Germany) became rapidly regularized. Of the many fascinating aspects of the early development of capitalistic foreign trade, we shall mention a few that are pertinent to our problem. Perhaps the most outstanding change which the growth of industry brought to England was the change from exporting raw materials and importing finished goods to the reverse process. Exporting finished goods, which, under the heavy fire of public opinion and government support, tended to create an active trade balance, increased the volume of precious metals available to English industry. England was very much in need of such an increase in the physical volume of its media of exchange, because the lack of precious metals compared to the increased volume of output of industrial commodities tended to depress prices for the latter without stimulating additional exports; for production depended on the availability of raw materials and labor rather than on a market demand, in this case an increase in the foreign demand. The result of insufficient exchange media was that the expansion of industry was delayed and the raw materials needed in addition to those available in England could not be bought in sufficient quantities.

Two metals were at that time especially fitted to serve as media of exchange: silver and gold. Silver existed in greater amounts, especially because of the intensive operation of mines in New Spain. Gold was scarcer, and because of its scarcity, it could not have served as the sole means of exchange during this period. Even combined with the existing silver supplies there was barely a sufficient quantity of both metals to satisfy the existing industrial and mercantile needs. Bimetallism, therefore, constituted a compromise on the part of the authorities concerned for the establishment of a relatively stable means of exchange.

We previously pointed out that bimetallism could not exist as early as the thirteenth and fourteenth centuries because there did not exist an automatically working relationship. The basis for such a mechanism was created in the rapidity of the interacting commercial transactions. If any one of the metals was overvalued or undervalued, the commercial transactions created an immediate reaction upon the other metal. This explains why bimetallism, as an *authoritatively* set up monetary system, was created in the United States and in smaller European countries rather than in England. Only where there were causes for continuous discrepancies between the two metals *on the basis of an outspoken scarcity of either one or both of the metals* do we find the creation of a government-secured standard of value by linking both metals *in a definite ratio.*

The development in England illustrates the point made above. England's trade expanded during the seventeenth and eighteenth centuries, and with it the need for an increased volume of currency. The silver flowing from America into Spain found its final destination in ever-greater quantities in the coffers of the merchants of England, enabling them not only to facilitate their transactions but also to satisfy the increasing need for a currency in small denominations. In the second half of the seventeenth century the trade with the East began to grow extraordinarily. The East India Company flourished on the basis of these new trade relations; their peculiar character was to have an extremely great influence upon the development of the English currency system. The main difficulty with this trade, whose economic character we may describe as one of the last revivals of trade capitalism, was that while England developed increasingly a taste for the wares of India, the Indians showed little desire for the purchase of English goods, especially English woolens.[4] The deficiency in the balance of payments in this trade was made up by the East India Company, whose export of silver, for which India showed an increasing demand, tended to relieve England of an excessive pressure on the ratio between gold and silver by depressing the price of silver. It is highly interesting to see how England, through this historical accident, was able to preserve a working balance in her bimetallic currency.

[4] *Ibid.,* p. 139.

While the East India trade offered an outlet for the surplus of silver, the developing manufacture in England was able to dispose of its output in Europe in exchange for considerable quantities of gold.

When Newton became Master of the Mint, silver had begun to show a tendency toward undervaluation with the result that small currency began to be scarce. When after the war with France gold began to flow into England, the government decided to decrease the price of the guinea, although the reduction in value to 21 shillings was not quite enough to offset entirely the overvaluation of gold. The result was a complete disappearance of all full-weight silver coins; [5] for all practical purposes gold supplanted silver as a standard of value. England thus "did not establish the gold standard by any conscious and deliberate act, and it is doubtful whether anyone foresaw that it would establish itself." [6]

To summarize, a monetary standard of value developed in England in the eighteenth century in terms of gold because the economic conditions created that standard. Silver remained in circulation to a certain extent, but it was valued according to the price of gold rather than as an independent medium of exchange.

BIMETALLISM AS A CONSCIOUSLY INTRODUCED GOVERNMENTAL MONETARY STANDARD   The setting of a government-secured ratio between gold and silver, that is, the establishment of a definite bimetallic standard, took place in the United States and France as well as in Latin countries. The colonial period of American economic development was characterized by two significant facts. First of all, America was taken into the European economic system as an appendage, as a source of supply for the raw-material needs of the mother country. In exchange, finished goods were exported to America. If any balances accrued in favor of England, they were to be transferred to England. Thus, there was no economic source either for the development or for the accumulation of money funds

5 Ibid., p. 142.   _6 Ibid._

in America except in so far as America engaged in economic activities unrelated to the English economic system.

The trade with Spanish America was here of outstanding importance. At the time of the War of Independence the prevailing means of exchange was the Spanish silver dollar, although the system of account was still the English one of shillings and pence. As there were no available sources of gold and silver in the United States or in the rest of North America, the young independent union was from the first faced with extraordinary difficulties in its attempt to establish a system of currency. This difficulty was increased by the spontaneous attempts to introduce paper currency, which met with disaster. The reason for this will be discussed in our chapter on paper currency. Hamilton's recommendation to Congress to adopt a bimetallic standard in 1792 constitutes, therefore, an attempt to bring order into the monetary chaos of the time and in doing so to use all the available metallic resources. The recourse to paper money was barred because of the circumstances indicated in the unfortunate experiences of the preceding period. It seemed to the economic theorists of the time that if a ratio between gold and silver were fixed, the automatic working of the bimetallic standard would insure that all changes in the market valuation of metal would lead finally to readjustments.

THE TECHNIQUE OF BIMETALLISM   The arguments of the advocates of bimetallism and the technique of the bimetallic standard as imagined by them were as follows: Contrasted with the existing scarcity of means of exchange, it was argued that two metals together would offer a broader base for currency and bank credit than either of them alone. The monetary unit was to be a weight of precious metals whereby one was replaceable, in terms of weight, by the other. Both metals were full legal tender, redemption possible in either metal, and both freely exportable and importable. If such a standard, with a mint ratio expressing the approximate market ratio of both metals at the time of introduction, were to be adopted, no danger was anticipated that either of the metals would disappear from the country. If, for instance, gold, because of an undervaluation in any country should leave that country, the scarcity thus created, invoked by the mint ratio, would produce a rise in its price, while the inflow of that gold into the other country would create there a relative abundance and accordingly depress its price. Thus a tendency would be created to equalize the values of gold and silver in both countries, and any deviatory movements would always tend to come to a halt.

The assumption in such a theoretical argument is that all other factors remain equal. As far as the United States was concerned, it was soon found out that in economic reality all other factors did not remain equal. Thus, for instance, the scarcity of precious metals in England led to the legal provision that Spanish dollars and other foreign coins could pass as legal tender as long as they were not below certain weights. As Spanish dollars had full weight, they were stopped by the American bankers and soon reappeared with a slight underweight instead of full weight. Spanish dollars acquired in the West Indies against lesser weight American dollars were melted down and presented to the American Mint, from which they emerged as an increased number of American dollars.

Supervision of the coinage of silver dollars was a result, not a cause, of the difficulties in the bimetallic standard as found in the inequalities of mint ratios in the different countries. France had decided to establish a bimetallic standard on the ratio of 15.5 to 1, while the American ratio was only 15 to 1. Only thirty-one years later the latter ratio was changed to approximately 16 to 1. In France the bimetallic standard had in practice been established in 1785. The coinage ratio of 15.5 to 1, legalized in 1803, expressed approximately the market ratio at that time. Soon, however, the silver became overvalued, and in America as well as in France silver was imported in large quantities. A reverse movement set in only in the late 1840's, after the discovery of new gold supplies.

France, as well as America, was thus, prior to the increase in the gold supply, practically on a silver standard, demonstrating that the attempt to broaden the currency basis by artificially linking two metal commodities had met with failure.

COINAGE   We dealt in the previous paragraphs predominantly with the problem of monetary standards, and before that with money in its exclusive aspect as a means of exchange. This was done in order to make it clear that the economic function of money cannot be derived directly from the particular physical forms. If we are going to deal now with concrete forms of the means of exchange, that is, first with coins and in the following chapter with paper money, we want to make it clear again that the economic function of these physical means of payments can be derived only from their character as commodities, which, because of certain characteristics are able to facilitate the exchange of all other commodities.

It has become commonplace to refer in any history of money to the etymology of our monetary terms. The terms "capital," "fee," and "pecuniary" in English, like the term "ruble" in Russian, are said to have been derived from terms for cattle. Innumerable examples undoubtedly can be quoted in support of the contention that cattle at certain times served as a means of exchange.[7] Aside from cattle we find cowrie shells, hoes, tea, pearls, knives, cloth, hides, and an endless array of other commodities used as means of exchange. The important point here is that each particular form of means of payment bore a direct relationship to the type of production in which it functioned. Early American history is especially rich in examples showing the validity of such a generalization. Thus, for instance, wampum was a perfect means of exchange for the Indians, "being a product of labor and subject to the law of supply and demand."[8] It served as a means of exchange for the colonists as long as their trade consisted mainly of exchange with the Indians. With the decline of the Indian

---

[7] For example, *Iliad* Book xxiii.
[8] Garis, *Principles of Money, Credit, and Banking*, p. 19.

beaver trade, this medium of exchange began to disappear, and beaver pelts themselves became the standard among the white trappers.[9] In other places other commodities were used. In New England we find musket bullets passing for a farthing apiece and acknowledged as legal tender at the current price, while in South Carolina rice performed the same function. Virginia used tobacco for this purpose.

The increase in the number as well as in the velocity of transactions made it desirable to have a means of exchange which was more easily divisible, more easily transportable, and less perishable than any one of the commodities here mentioned. It was found that metals have these characteristics in the highest degree; of copper, iron, tin, silver, and gold, the two latter gradually developed into a predominant position, because they were sufficiently scarce to reduce the actual weight in the exchange transactions to a minimum.

We have referred above to the relation between silver and gold in England in the seventeenth and the eighteenth centuries. The disappearance of silver and the consequent shortage of money of smaller denominations for purposes of exchange had led to considerable import of less valuable foreign coins and to the production of counterfeit pieces. It is interesting that these counterfeit and foreign coins did not influence the value of the currency, since they assumed the function of token money, that is, means for fractional payments, thus merely filling the gap which the disappearance of silver money had created.

The great difficulty with the token money was its regulation, especially because the technique of coining was but slightly developed. When, between 1717 and 1754, the government coined copper for small denominations, copper soon began to disappear, as silver had disappeared. Adam Smith suggested

---

[9] An interesting development at this time was the introduction of a "super standard" known as the "Plew." The "Plew" was an exceptionally fine beaver skin possessing a superiority so easily recognized that it brought a premium in exchange. The etymology of the term is interesting and simple. It was merely a phonetic spelling on the part of the American trappers of the French word *plus* which was used first in this connection by the Canadian trappers of French origin.

increasing the price of silver and making it legal tender only in payments up to one guinea.[10] In France and elsewhere in Europe the same difficulties were encountered.

PAPER MONEY AND THE EMERGENCE OF COUNTRY BANKING

With paper currency more than any other form in which currency had appeared up to that time there was a temptation to forget that all money is only a means of exchange and *as such bound to a definite system of production.* Most historical accounts of the development of money refer to long genealogies of the bank note, the draft, the bill of exchange, the letter of credit, and in their quest for origin stop only short of prehistoric times. While it is probably true that certain forms developed in certain periods of history have reappeared in other periods of history, it is important to realize that the functions of these forms changed radically.

In the period with which we are mainly concerned here, that of England at the time of the Industrial Revolution, we find that two separate systems of paper currency were in use and that little occasion existed, at least in the beginning, for them to cross each other's paths. The Bank of England was founded in 1694 for the double purpose of providing the government with an effective instrument for public loans, and to serve the London merchants as an investment and exchange institution.[11] The important thing to keep in mind here is the character of the trade in which the London merchants were

[10] Smith, *Wealth of Nations,* I, 20.

[11] Andreades, *History of the Bank of England;* Feavearyear, *The Pound Sterling;* W. T. C. King, *History of the London Discount Market;* Godfrey, *A Brief Account of the Intended Bank of England; An Appeal to the People of England, the Public Companies and Monied Interests on the Renewal of the Charter of the Bank;* A Gentleman of the Bank, *The Bank of England's Vade Mecum, or, Sure guide* . . . in which every office, place, and the manner of procuring notes of every sort for cash is distinctly described; Committee of Secrecy, *Report,* 1797; Committee of Secrecy, *Report Feb. 26, 1797;* Atkinson, *Considerations on the Propriety of the Bank of England Resuming Its Payments in Specie; The Bank—the Stock Exchange—the Bankers —the Bankers Clearing House—the Minister, and the Public;* Verax (i.e., Richard Groom), *The Bank of England Defended, or The Principal Cause of the High Prices Demonstrated;* Acres, *The Bank of England from Within;* Feavearyear, *Banking and Finance in Europe and U.S.*

engaged. As we have mentioned before, England experienced at that time a last wave of trade capitalism, that is, an economic system predominantly interested in the transfer of commodities and, at least as far as London was concerned, interested only in a secondary degree, if at all, in the production of the goods in which they were trading. This was possible only as long as production continued on a handicraft or semi-handicraft basis. As soon as the yield of the putting-out system began to limp behind the needs for new production and steam power replaced the power of human hands, larger investments became necessary not only for the payment of wages but also for raw material outlays which would be returned to the merchants financing production after the manufactured products were sold. There were in addition new machines bought, whose value in the form of depreciation charges was returned to the investor only over a long period of time.

The other aspect of the process shows that concentration of laborers under one roof, necessitated by the introduction of machines, had transplanted the worker into the towns and thus removed him from the source of a large part of his income, the land. Supplies which he thus forfeited had to be replaced by increased purchases in the towns, and the process of democratizing demand, which we have referred to previously, received a decisive impetus. Where was the means of exchange for the multitude of these transactions to come from? Previously, the merchant had given the handicraft man the raw materials. Now he had to enable the producers to buy machines and to pay the increased number of workers, the latter now wholly dependent upon their remuneration for the re-creation of their energies. We have referred above to the state of coinage and to the availability of precious metals. We have to add now that while trade capitalism had concentrated in London, new production was necessarily developing in the country. Here the absence of adequate means of communication and transportation would have decreased the usefulness of precious metals even if they had been available. Land transport was still being carried on by means of pack horses.

The first coach road reached Liverpool in 1760. When the traffic in goods increased, the greater part of them was sent over canals, the building of which had begun by 1720.[12] The way out of this difficulty was found both in the close co-operation of the country merchants and the producers and in the increased volume of purchasing transactions per unit of money. Merchants were able to grant credits to the producers, but the form of these credits had to be such as to enable the producers to pay for their machines as well as to pay the wages of their laborers. To fill this need country banking and paper money of small denominations came into existence.[13]

The paper money thus created has to be definitely distinguished from the bills of exchange which trade capitalism had developed earlier. However, even the latter began to take on new characteristics. With the development of the trade between Liverpool and Boston and Philadelphia, which was considerably aided by the greatly increased risk on the South coast of England because of continuing wars, the center of large-scale trade began to shift away from London. The attempts of the London merchants to retain their predominance was reflected in the struggle between the Bank of England and the banking houses in the provinces engaged in this new trade. The regularity of the Liverpool trade made it possible to employ the bill of exchange,[14] and, because of this, Liverpool was able to make itself independent of the bullion accumulated in London. This antagonism between the two types of trade, or rather production, is thus behind the "battle of bullion versus bills."

Thus, the development of paper money, the coining of

[12] Hughes, *Liverpool Banks and Bankers; a history of the circumstances which gave rise to the industry, and of the men who founded and developed it,* pp. 4–5.

[13] Phillips, *A History of Banks, Bankers, and Banking in Northumberland, Durham, and North Yorkshire.*

[14] The periods over which the bills ran varied greatly, according to the length of the voyages of the merchant ships, from 90 days sight to 42 month date. Generally these bills would be drawn against commodities. Such bills were frequently sold by public auction (*cf.,* Hughes, *Liverpool Banks and Bankers,* p. 41).

metals, as well as the role and the movement of precious metals, can be understood only through their function as a means of exchange within the economic mechanism of a given period.

3 · The Genesis of Banking

U P to this point we have followed one aspect of the development of money, as a means of exchange, and predominantly for finished goods. It has been indicated, however, that the developing industrial system created some new needs which money had to fulfill. In the preceding period of relatively pure trade capitalism, production was carried on by means of handicraft labor. The tools needed in this production were provided by the master and in most cases were produced by the master's establishment. With the change from handicraft to manufacture, and especially from manufacture to small-scale industrial enterprise, increasing division of labor brought on the need for the creation of producers' goods industries.

INDUSTRIAL CREDIT   The result was that in order to begin productive operations an initial capital became increasingly necessary.[1] This was needed, first, to buy the machines needed for production and, secondly, to pay wages until the time when the return on the goods sold should begin to flow back to the enterprise. With the division between trade and production, the need for a new source of this capital became increasingly felt. It can be observed that historically the inventions which characterized the beginnings of the Industrial Revolution coincided with the first formulation of this problem of obtaining necessary money capital in the monetary

[1] As to the size of the volume of capital existing then, various estimates have been made (see Sir R. Giffen, *The Growth of Capital*). Sir William Petty believed the total capital of England in 1679 to be about 250 million pounds, computed on the basis of a national income of 40 million pounds. Professor W. R. Scott (*The Constitution and Finance of . . . Joint Stock Companies to 1720*, I, 265) computes the rate of growth of this capital as one and one-half million pounds per year, *i.e.*, 1½ percent, which nearly coincides with the estimate of Gregory King for the year 1664 (1¼ percent). The part assessed to manufacturing capital was very small: 31 million pounds out of the total of 250 million pounds. The reliability of these figures is, however, of a rather doubtful character, as especially the figures for manufacture and trade may have been underestimations for the purpose of protection "from the hands of the rapacious tax gatherers" (Lord, *Capital and Steam-Power, 1750–1800*, p. 62).

theory of the "Invisible College," for example, by David Hume.[2]

The rate of economic expansion in this period had left the rate of increase in the volume of precious metals far behind. The advantages of machine production were too obvious, however, to be left unused because of this scarcity. The markets were there, and all that was necessary was to produce the commodities. It was under these conditions that credit in the form of bank notes was created. The merchant who was acquainted with the market conditions was willing to help the producer with the process of production in his own—the merchant's—interest. The producer needed to acquire raw materials and to pay wages. To satisfy the merchant's need for monetary facilities for acquiring wholesale raw materials, the already existing bill of exchange began to serve this new purpose.[3] For the payment of wages the local merchants issued notes on their own credit in favor of the producers.[4] These notes were more readily accepted by the public than notes which the individual factories might have issued, because the merchant houses were better known. Although anyone "who could persuade people to trust him, was at liberty to issue paper of the nature of bank notes, and as much of it as he pleased. . . . A hundred years ago there was no weekly drawing out of the bank of what was wanted for wages . . ."[5] There "arose a class of man, trader or merchant, who acted as bankers to the community, still retaining a separate business. The date 1760 is not an exact, but a convenient, date to indicate the period of the rise of bankers."[6] Moreover, "no bank came into existence as such all at once."[7] Another reason for the issuing of notes by the merchants can be found in the often neglected fact that by means of these notes they were able to obtain control over the goods produced. As the basic indus-

---

[2] See pp. 46–52, 61.　　　　　　　[3] See p. 26.

[4] "Paper, representing amounts which no one would today think of paying except in coin, was the financier's medium in almost all ordinary trade transactions, and people were glad to have it" (see Grindon, *Manchester Banks and Bankers; Historical Biographical and Anecdotal*, p. 32).

[5] *Ibid.*, p. 33.　　　　　　　[6] Hughes, *Liverpool Banks and Bankers*, p. iv.

[7] *Ibid.*, p. vii.

tries in England were located in the country, the development
which we describe here is generally known as "the development of the country banks." As early as August, 1755, Bell,
Cookson, Carr, and Airey, of New Castle, later known as Sir
Matthew White Ridley and Company, were issuing their own
notes.[8] These early banking transactions were carried on in
some obscure corner of the still-prevailing merchant business.
A "substantial portion of the business consisted in the discounting of small acceptances and promises-to-pay." [9] The
increasing needs for credit soon made it necessary for these
banking merchants to establish connections with London
bankers on whom they could draw. Smaller merchants asked
larger merchants who had been able to establish such connections with London to accommodate them through the
accounts which the latter had opened with their well-established reputations. The discounting and the negotiating of
bills, of which we shall speak in more detail below, was soon
added to the transactions of the banking departments of the
merchant houses. In a short time the latter found that they
were carrying on in this one department a volume of business
which in many cases began to dominate the original trading
aspect of the firm. Another step in the development was
reached when these departments finally grew independent,

---

[8] *A History of Banks, Bankers, and Banking in Northumberland, Durham,
and North Yorkshire*, p. 24. Or to give another vivid example of this process:
"Before the commencement of our local banking, Manchester had become a
great centre for the advantageous disposal of agricultural produce [*i.e.*, when
the crowding of people into factories, and that is into towns had begun.
KHN]. The Lancashire and Cheshire farmers, and the Yorkshire graziers very
particularly, were accustomed to come here in their strength. Coin being
scarce, like other country dealers of the period, they paid and received the
heaviest part of their accounts in paper-money. After 1770, on arrival in
Manchester, they resorted either to one of the banks . . . or to some friend
who would help them after banking fashion. This friend was often the landlord of a tavern, the bar-parlour serving as a kind of a primitive clearing-
house. . . . Here the various notes and drafts were sorted and exchanged,
the landlord assisting with coin, and finding an excellent opportunity for
doing a little discounting the while he supplied nicotian and congenerous
sources of comfort. . . . Mr. Thomas Mottram was such a landlord. Owner
of the Fox 'a celebrated old house of call,' 1810, he acquired an interest in a
cotton factory, becomes a banker purely and solely."—Grindon, *Manchester
Banks and Bankers*, pp. 71–72.
[9] Grindon, *Manchester Banks and Bankers*, p. 32.

either by separating from the original merchant business or by eliminating it entirely.

The size of such country banks was necessarily limited. By the Act of 1708, which renewed the charter of the Bank of England, the number of partners in all other banking firms had been limited to six. In the face of the increasing capital needs, this limitation became a serious handicap in the development of country banking.

James and Jonathan Backhouse and Company are perhaps typical of the development of such country banks. James and his son Jonathan were originally linen and worsted manufacturers in Darlington. They had extended to traders, manufacturers, and farmers of their neighborhood the various accommodations of a banking business, until they established, in 1774, a regular bank. The first note issue was restricted to one-guinea and five-guinea notes. These were followed by notes for one, five, ten, and twenty pounds. By careful regulation of their stocks of specie, they were able to handle all their business and to withstand the runs on country banks which were not infrequent during this pioneer stage of banking development. They finally established branches in Sunderland, Durham, New Castle, and Stockton.[10]

Once again we call attention to the fact that the notes issued served predominantly the local needs of a growing industry. They were issued on the basis of the confidence of the local public in the older merchant houses and, conversely, because of the confidence of these merchant houses in particular industries. It is therefore irrelevant to observe that the Bank of England had been issuing notes ever since its foundation in 1694. This bank and its notes could not possibly fulfill the function of the notes issued by the country banks, because branches of the Bank of England did not exist until much later in the country, and without close contact no such note issue on the basis of an intimate knowledge of the actual economic conditions could have taken place. Secondly, and more important, is the point that the notes of the Bank of England

10 *Ibid.*, p. 131.

were fulfilling at the time of the creation of the country bank notes quite a different function from the one which we have ascribed to the latter class.[11]

The volume of the notes issued by the country banks was delimited only by the needs for credit on the one hand and the ability to rediscount them if necessary on the other. Specie was important only in times of stress, when, in a run on the banks, the public among whom the notes were circulating wanted to see "real values," though "in the times of the unreasonable and unreasoning occurrences called 'panics,' it is not so much the holders of notes who do the mischief as the depositors, and these now behaved like lunatics" (that is, 1797).[12] Otherwise, specie was only necessary in small amounts to meet the average daily needs. The subscribed capital of most of the banks was necessarily limited because of the restriction in the number of partners. No legal limitation, however, was put on the volume of notes issued.

From the statements made in the time of the panic of 1793, we learn that the collective issue of four of the New Castle banks was 250,000 pounds (an average of 62,500 pounds each); that the Durham bank (Mills Hopper and Company) had an issue of 31,420 pounds, and Messrs. Bell, Woodall, and Company, 25,000 pounds. Besides the four New Castle banks mentioned above there were eighteen issuing-banks carrying on business at this time. If we estimate that they had an average issue of 25,000 pounds each, which would certainly be within the mark, we reach a note issue of 450,000 pounds; if we add to this the issue of the four New Castle banks which is known to have been 230,000 pounds, there appears to have been a total of 680,000 pounds of notes in circulation.[13]

To repeat our earlier statement, the money thus created was not used in the first instance as a means of exchange, but as a means of creating the needed additional capital, the automatic formation of which, in absence of proper institutions and because of the still unfinished integration, was lagging

---

[11] See p. 15.   [12] Grindon, *Manchester Banks and Bankers*, p. 76.
[13] Phillips, *A History of Banks, Bankers, and Banking in Northumberland*, pp. 57–59.

behind the demands of the expanding productive structure of the country. These new banks were therefore, as far as their actual function in the process of production was concerned, primarily financing institutions and have to be distinguished, therefore, from earlier institutions of a different character for example, the Bank of England, the earlier goldsmiths, and the still earlier Fugger Banks.[14] Until the time of the Industrial Revolution there had been no need for this new type of financial institution. Only now the power-driven machinery which had made large-scale production possible necessitated the creation of short-term credit. One reason that these banking institutions developed in the country lies in the fact that the lack of adequate means of communication still separated the centers of production from the money market of the Trade Era in London. More important, however, is that the London bankers would not have been able to supply the needs for discounts, since they administered only the spare cash of the merchants and the rents of the landlords.

Aside from the industrial function of these new banking institutions, agriculture developed an increasing need for capital investment from the outside. The new program of intensive agriculture, necessitated by the rapid development of large populations concentrated in the industrial areas, required means which hardly could be supplied from the rent-income of the landowners. Here, again, the local banker knew the local agricultural producer and was in a position to satisfy his capital wants. We can sum up, then, by saying that the country banks "were in the main the offspring of the Industrial Revolution." [15]

We have said previously that the function of the Bank of England and the London banks in general was quite different from that of the country banks, but this functional difference did not prevent the acts passed in connection with the administration and the policy of the Bank of England from having a considerable effect on the country banks. We have

---

[14] Cf. Richards, *The Early History of Banking in England;* also Ehrenberg, *Capital and Finance in the Age of the Renaissance.*

[15] Feavearyear, *The Pound Sterling,* p. 149.

already referred to the fact that the Act of 1708, limiting the size of all banks except the Bank of England to not more than six partners, proved to be a serious handicap in the development of country banking. This was even more true of the acts subsequently passed. The country banks flourished under the Bank Restriction Act of 1796 for the reason that while the Act was in effect payment of cash for notes was not compulsory. This expansion was curbed by the Act of 1804, which limited the life of a country bank note to three years from the date of issue. To understand the passage of such an act and its subsequent change, we must realize that the progress in the industrialization of the country made itself felt also in the improvement of the means of communication. The close contact between the country bank and its clientele was seriously threatened by the growth of the country banks and the extension of their scope of business far beyond that sphere which previously had been determined by the absence of means of communication. The type of confidence which had resulted from the close contact between the country banker and the producer-clientele was thus disturbed, and the note issue became again temporarily insecure until new and adequate institutions were developed.

The increase in the scope of country bank business, however, proved to be the most effective check on its own expansion. Country banks were built upon capital invested directly by the owners of the bank. The increasing needs for bank capital could not be adequately supplied by these bankers personally. The time was ripe for the development of joint stock banking, the basis of which lies in the subscription of capital owned by people not participating in any respect in the management of the bank and interested only in the interest paid on the investment. We witness at this stage the birth of absentee ownership of bank capital. Before we investigate further this structural change in the functioning of banks, we will direct our attention to another aspect in the development of money in early industrial society, the development of commercial credit instruments.

COMMERCIAL CREDIT We have already referred to the fact that the increase in industrial output was not only accompanied by an increase in the volume of consumer demand on the home market, but also and necessarily by an increase in the volume of foreign trade. The Bank of England had been established as a purely mercantile institution. The economic function of the merchants who bought the initial stock of the Bank of England consisted in the transfer of commodities irrespective of where and how they were produced. In this connection it is of incidental interest to know that the charter for the Bank of England was granted because of the need of the government for new credits to insure the protection desired by the merchants. While it is true that during the early part of the eighteenth century purely mercantile business began to decrease and the importance of the Bank of England was maintained because of its function as a credit-creating institution for the government, there is little evidence that the governors of the Bank of England realized that an entirely new money function was developing in Liverpool in its trade with Philadelphia and Baltimore, over which they had actually little control.

This "Age of Liverpool" [16] marks a definite change in the character of foreign trade. Before the middle of the sixteenth century English foreign trade had been staple trade, and its main problem had been to avoid changes in the value of money caused by the "clipping" of the coins by the government. Between 1550 and 1650 England developed the putting-out system, which enabled her to begin the export of finished goods. The raw materials necessary for this production were available in ample quantities within the country. Between 1650 and 1750 the productivity of England increased because of the concentration of production in manufacturing establishments. The raw materials needed by English industry began to exceed the resources of the country and import became imperative. This gradual shift in the character of foreign trade has to be kept in mind if we wish to disentangle the

16 Newbold, *Democracy, Debts, and Disarmament,* pp. 16 ff.

otherwise confusing, if not contradictory, doctrines of the whole mercantile era. Up to the middle of the seventeenth century, the money problem in international trade consisted in the avoidance of too-rapid price changes because of the irregular increase in the value of precious metals as compared with the still slow but distinct increase in the volume of trade. With the increase in trade brought about by the increase in output, the problem of money took on an entirely new aspect. Money was now not only a medium of exchange between English raw materials and foreign finished goods but also a means for acquiring the necessary factors of production. It is at this moment that the possession of bullion receives significance for production. Acquisition of more precious metals meant now the ability to buy more raw materials, and to sell more finished goods meant to get more precious metals. Selling more finished goods was possible only by increasing raw material imports, and the larger these were, the less of the available purchasing power for foreign goods was spent on the importation of foreign "luxury" goods. Concomitantly, it was advocated to keep wages, that is, the cost of production, low so that the home-produced goods were available for exportation. From these few principles we can deduce most of the prevailing theories on population, the effectiveness of labor, factory organization, taxation, and so forth. Most important, however, for the problem at hand, was the acquisition of foreign purchasing power.

The form of this purchasing power depended to a considerable extent upon the concrete form which the trade relations assumed at a given time. Precious metals were required only while the relations were still of an arbitrary and insecure character. To the degree that these relations became regular, we see that the need for concrete money decreased more or less parallel with the continuously proven correctness of the anticipated payments. In the relationship between Liverpool and Baltimore and Boston, we can observe for the first time just how such a regular intercourse creates its own form of money, that is, the bill of exchange. It is true that bills of exchange had been used at various times in history, but it was at this time that they became an integral part of the economic process. On both sides of the Atlantic, but more especially in England, discount houses began to appear whose main function was to finance this import of raw materials against the export of finished goods. These discount houses, plus the country banks, were the institutions characteristic of the first phase of industrial England.

The function of the Bank of England had been to provide the monetary mechanism for premanufacture and industrial trade traffic. To the degree that this type of trade traffic declined in importance and the new foreign trade increased, a conflict had to develop between the discount houses and the Bank of England, which was the more serious because the monetary function of the Bank of England had become increasingly allied with the function of government. "London against Liverpool" means the struggle of bullion against bills, and the cumulative volume of the latter was a thrust in consequence of which the Bank of England began to interest itself in the traffic in bills and the discount houses began to invade the London money market.

4 · The Quantity Doctrine of Bullionism

MERCANTILISM AND THE CONCEPT OF WEALTH In preceding chapters we have referred to that preindustrial phase of economic development which commonly goes under the heading "mercantilism." While in medieval times the soil had served as the focus for whatever economic thinking did exist, with the progress of manufacture soil tended to be replaced and labor assumed increased importance. If, therefore, we try to analyze mercantilist thought in relation to its concept of wealth, we shall find that its definition centered on labor and expressed thus the main problem with which the production system was confronted. In this respect mercantilist thinkers did only what later economists have done in their respective times. For instance, after the putting-out system changed into a relatively well-established factory system they presented the problem of relative scarcity of labor in the form of the theory of labor value, which, in comparison to the seemingly crude physical concept of labor of the mercantilists, amounted to an adequate and functional formulation of their main problem.

The concept "wealth" always refers to the productive activity of society. Production on an enlarged scale and on higher levels presupposed, however, that the necessary factors of production were obtainable. This was particularly true for the period which preceded the introduction of the steam engine. The most important economic factor at the turn of the eighteenth century was the need for labor capable of producing manufactured products; labor still largely existed only in its dormant state of agricultural semi-serf labor. To make labor available for manufacture, it was necessary to transform it into free labor, that is, into a commodity which could be bought according to need and which had to be educated to be able to perform manufacturing services. The development in Russia so much commented upon in recent times demonstrates well the difficulties confronting a semi-serf and agricultural society when it is in process of changing into an industrial society. The difficulties encountered in the process of re-educating labor were considerable, and we find the economists of the manufacturing period concentrating upon educational expositions, the enormous value of which seems to us difficult to realize. Again we observe that statements of the theorists are made only after the material content of their expositions exists in social reality.

In the difficulties which the expanding manufacturing economy experienced because of the lagging supply of its main factor of production we find determined the fundamental position of what later was termed the "mercantile theory of investment." By "investment" is meant here the process of employing available factors of production for the purpose of expanding that existing production. The problem of acquiring and transferring these factors of production, that is, the monetary function as such, was not overlooked, but it should be clearly brought out that the need for money capital in that period was secondary to the actual physical existence of the factors of production without which money capital could not change into investment.

Jacob Viner remarked in his classical critical investigation into the period of transition from mercantilism to industrialism that the confusion of the mercantilists has a tendency to persist in modern times. It may also be said that there is a definite trend in modern writings concerning the mercantile period to inject our confusion about our own economic reality into the interpretation of the earlier economic thought. It is, for example, of relatively small importance to point out that previous investigators into the development of the function of money have divided the history of mercantilism into two distinct periods. Viner recounts as the reasons for such a distinction:

(1) that, before 1620, stress was put on the importance of a favorable balance in each transaction of each merchant, whereas, in the later period the emphasis was on the aggregate or national balance of trade; (2) that, before 1620, concern about the state of the individual balances was due to the anxiety that the country's store of bullion *be not reduced,* whereas in the later period, there was

anxiety that *it be increased;* (3) that, before 1620, the chief economic objective of trade policy was to protect the national currency against exchange depreciation, whereas after 1620, this was
a minor objective, if a matter of concern at all; (4) that, in the
early period, the means advocated and employed to carry out the
objective of the prevailing trade policy were close regulation of
the transactions of particular individuals in the exchange market
and in coin and bullion, while in the later period the policy
recommended and put into practice was to seek the objective of
a greater stock of bullion indirectly by means of regulation of
trade rather than directly through restriction on exchange transactions and on the export of coin and bullion.[1]

It is perfectly true that many of the customs and legal restrictions of the earlier period prevailed long after 1620, while
others had been proposed, if not enacted and used earlier than
1620. The difficulty is solved if we conceive of *economic institutions* not only as being in flux but also as not changing their
legal superstructures and some correlative ways until long
after the laws and the theoretical formulations have become
obsolete.

We have grown accustomed to recognizing the period of
mercantilism by its concept of wealth. This wealth was presented as being created by an excess of exports over imports.
This doctrine meant in the early period of mercantilism that
the gradual expansion of trade, originally made possible by
the development of manufacture, encountered as its main
obstacle the lack of a proportionally increasing fund of means
of exchange. As has been pointed out previously, this relative
lack of means of exchange was crucially important in this
period, because the social basis for its alleviation by means of
credit did not yet fully exist. Credit, and that means in this
connection also all kinds of fiduciary money, presupposes the
existence of normal transactions: "normal" in this case being
commercial transactions which take place regularly.[2] It thus
becomes evident that in this pioneer stage of international

---

[1] Viner, *Studies in the Theory of International Trade,* pp. 3–4.
[2] The development within a country and between countries is not necessarily contemporaneous. The use of credit for the financing of national trade
and production is noticeable in England in the early part of the sixteenth
century; see Wilson, *A Discourse upon Usury,* pp. 43 ff.

trade-capitalism the merchants were not concerned with the
relation between an existing volume of money and the value
expression of a coexisting volume of commodities. To take
such a position would have presupposed the existence of a
generally adequate volume of money, that is, adequate to the
volume of commodity-exchange to be transacted, and this
money must have existed in the form of bullion because of the
absence of any appreciable concrete possibilities for credit.
The fact was that the productive capabilities of England as
well as the opportunities for trade were far outdistancing the
available bullion.

MONEY AND INVESTMENT   For what concrete purpose, then,
was this bullion needed? The gradual growth of manufacture
became very distinct in the sixteenth century. The outstanding problem was to secure the means with which to produce,
that is, capital; especially since England herself was poor in
natural supplies of the precious metals. The urgency of this
problem in the form of hard money as well as credit pervades
the history of prices and public finance of that time. The
possibility of disposing of finished commodities abroad seemed
to open to England a way to procure the bullion so badly
needed for its production. To acquire wealth meant to be able
to produce, and in order to produce one had to be able to sell
in order to receive the means for production. Here, as every-
where, we find exemplified in a classical form the fact that
history does not proceed in the form of causal chains but as
an interdependent process.

Johnson remarks that

Behind the doctrine that credit items in a nation's balance of
payments could be increased by exporting manufactured goods
. . . lay a medieval theory of value: that value can, should, and
does increase in relation to the amount of labor which has been
expended in the improvement of commodities.[3]

He refers here to the theory of the *justum pretium* of St.
Thomas Aquinas. There is, however, little connection be-

[3] Johnson, *Predecessors of Adam Smith*, p. 304.

tween the theory of St. Thomas, which was designed to rationalize away the need for interest in middle Europe, and the beginnings of the theory of labor value, which was formulated in quite different circumstances and which referred to the fact that economic energy priced in terms of the necessities for its maintenance had assumed primary importance in the performance of production. We are here concerned with the means of transfer of factors within the process of production; while the argument of St. Thomas was used only as a vehicle to express the fact that to increase production, money capital was necessary for the hiring of labor and the buying of tools, as well as for the payment for raw materials and the payment for royalties. This necessary money capital could be obtained only by exchanging labor for it. And it was mentioned before that this money capital took the form of bullion. As Viner said, "the mercantilists . . . wanted more money because they regarded money not merely as a passive means of exchange but as a force, acting through its circulation from hand to hand, as an active stimulus to trade." [4] The identity between money as a circulating medium and capital as a prerequisite for production is during this time a real one and by no means only a confusion.[5] Even in the various attempts to discuss the role of interest we find an interesting reflection of the prevailing conditions surrounding the functioning of money as capital during this time.[6]

The assumption of confusion in the writings of the early mercantilists arises mainly from the use of a terminology which in its conceptual content refers to the period preceding mercantilism. The outgoing Middle Ages and the early period of mercantilism have in common a preoccupation with trade. An analysis which does not take into account the fundamental difference in the character of the trade in these two periods and in neglecting this basic difference takes the term "trade" to mean in both cases the same thing must necessarily lead to an apparent confusion, that is, lead to false conclusions. At

[4] Viner, *Studies in the Theory of International Trade,* p. 36.
[5] Cf. *ibid.,* p. 31.   [6] See pp. 68 ff.

the end of the Middle Ages the middle European merchants were predominantly carriers of oriental goods; they only gradually took over the trading of European manufactured products. The consumers of the commodities in the earlier trading were exclusively the courts, the clergy, the army, and to a negligible extent, if considered in relation to the other groups, the merchants themselves. In early mercantilism, the merchants became to an increasing extent more intimately connected with production, if not identified with it. The consumers were by no means only members of the court, but the growing number of producers and traders as well as the swelling multitude of journeymen and the army, which had changed its nature with the development of national states.[7]

MERCANTILISM AND "QUANTITY OF MONEY"   Preoccupation with acquiring bullion has to be understood as part of the setting of an expanding manufacturing economy, in which the scarce means of exchange were being secured by export of produced commodities. We also find that under these conditions there was no cause for the formulation of what later was called a "quantity theory of money."[8] A direct relation between volume of money and volume of commodities can be established only if we presuppose the existence of at least a quasi-static relation of the data within the equation. If there is a continuous quantitative change on either side, or if it can be shown that for reasons indigenous to the process of production both sides change quantitatively at a disproportionate

[7] While we are discussing the form and the language in which many of the early mercantilists wrote, we may say a few words on the much used and frequently criticised analogy to personal finance. Whether an analogy from the general, that is, the economic system, to the particular, that is, the economic individual, will hold or not, does not rest on absolute and eternally logical grounds, but depends entirely on the concrete relation of the general to the particular at the time under consideration. As we shall point out later, in our discussion of the quantity theory of money, it is our opinion that in the period of industrial expansion—and this period began with the period of manufacture, that is, the period which we usually call mercantilism—the individual unit of the new type of production was representative of the whole new type of production. Structurally, there was no difference between the economic actions of an individual, and economic activity in general.

[8] Angell, *The Theory of International Prices,* pp. 13 ff.

rate, the formulation of quantity equations between money and prices has no point. It is for this reason, also, that we find little discussion among the theorists of this time concerning price inflation. The notion "inflation," simply having a primary relevance to price changes in the domestic economy, had little, if any, meaning in the economic reality of that period. Many economic historians have linked the scarcity or abundance of precious metals directly to their physical availability. There is no doubt that the mere physical presence or absence of precious metals can cause noticeable inflations or deflations under certain conditions. It would, however, oversimplify the conditions prevailing in the late sixteenth and the first half of the seventeenth century to attempt to explain the gradual lessening in the intensity of the bullionist argument from Hales via Locke to David Hume by attributing it simply to a decrease in the physical scarcity of the means of exchange. As we have discussed before, it was during this time that the various means of credit developed, and in developing gradually lessened the intensity of the demand for "hard" money, even though the rise of industry increased the demand for means of exchange. To repeat, this was possible only because of the gradual but definite growth of a regular manufacturing economy. With the changing economic circumstances, the classic formulation of the quantity theory of money was only very gradually approximated by various writers of that time. Malynes observed "that plentie of money maketh generally things deare, and scarcitie of money maketh likewise generally things good cheape." [9] Mun said, "It is common saying, that plenty or scarcity of money makes all things dear or good or cheap." [10]

The transition from a definite bullionistic point of view to a quantity theory position is well exemplified by William Potter, who noticed that an increase of money in circulation may produce a more than equal increase in manufacture and trade. Potter observes, quite correctly for this time, that fast

[9] Gerard de Malynes, "A Treatise of the Canker of England's Commonwealth," *Tudor Economic Documents*, III, 387.

[10] Thomas Mun, *England's Treasure by Forraign Trade*, p. 28.

sales made possible because of the availability of money enable manufacturers to produce more, thus making it possible for them to reduce the prices for the commodities, not to increase them, as the quantity theory maintained. When money became available in a volume adequate to meet the demand, this phenomenon began to disappear. If previously the fluctuations in the supply of money had consisted of the ups and downs of scarce precious metals, then an increase in the supply of money, that is, bullion, after a balance between supply of bullion and demand for it had been reached, meant an increase beyond what was needed at this moment by production. This oversupply then necessarily influenced the money price of the produced commodities.

The transition is even more pronounced in the argument of James Hodges.[11] He granted that an increase in the volume of money may result in a rise of prices, but this rise would come about only after the increase in the volume of money had acted as a means to further production. This argument is still quite different from Hume's theory that an increase in price may act as a stimulus for trade. While sounding alike, the writers had different aspects of economic life in mind. Hodges was still interested in alleviating the difficulties of production, while Hume was already concerned with the problem of distribution, which he assumed would then react positively on production.

It was only toward the end of the seventeenth century that the idea seems to have gained ground that there is a "due proportion" between commodities and money, and that for this reason there exists the possibility that there may be too much or too little of the one or the other. Sir William Petty, for instance, said that "there may be as well too much money in a country, as too little. I mean, as to the best advantage of its trade; only the remedy is very easy, it may be soon turned into the magnificence of gold and silver vessels." [12] Others, such as Vanderlint and Houghton, expressed the same problem in

---

11 Hodges, *The Present State of England as to Coin and Publick Charges.*
12 Petty, "The Political Anatomy of Ireland," in *Economic Writings,* 1, 193.

similar terms, namely, that there may be a possibility of having too much bullion, that is, money, this "too much" causing unfavorable reactions upon the price level.

The puzzle with which interpreters of economic doctrines have been confronted in trying to harmonize the views of the earlier and later mercantilists, therefore, dissolves itself. Hoarding is a vice as long as that which is hoarded is scarce and badly needed. As soon as the demand for it is adequately taken care of, the previous vice turns, if not into virtue, into something at least indifferent in character.

STATE FINANCE Historically, as well as functionally, the establishment of an economy of manufacture on the basis of free labor coincided with the final stage in the formation of national states. It would go beyond the limits set for our study to trace in detail this development. It must suffice to say that the growing tendency to delegate economic duties to the state, aggressive as well as protective in character, brought about serious financial problems. With the fifteenth century public finance gradually acquired an entirely new meaning, although in name and legal terminology the king's household continued to administer the finances of the maturing nation. His personality had transcended his physical existence.[13] "Le roi est mort, vive le roi" was a slogan indicating that the debts incurred by one king were to be assumed by his successor. The changed sources of his income caused the active control over the nation's income as well as over its expenditures, and over the degree to which it was allowed to incur liabilities, to pass to the merchants, who in the putting-out system had been changing into part-producers. The crown thus became the active instrument of the new economic society. When this economy expanded, and this expansion was accompanied by a continued series of war-like emergencies, it became clear that not only basic production and its resultant distributive apparatus were sorely in need of more bullion but also the state itself developed an urgent demand for adequate means

[13] Ehrenberg, *Capital and Finance in the Age of the Renaissance*, pp. 32 ff.

to pay for these never-ending emergencies. This, in turn, meant that the state needed to accumulate bullion. This problem of accumulation of state treasure is discussed by the mercantilists in all its varied aspects. Mun, for instance, admonishes the princes to be frugal on the one side, while on the other, he warns that no more treasure should be added annually than would result from the excess of exports over imports.

SAVING IN THE FORM OF BULLION AND INVESTMENT   Much has been written about the idea of the mercantilists that precious metals were a store of wealth. While this contention was undoubtedly true for the mercantilists, it can be understood only in connection with the purpose for which wealth is saved at a given time. Opportunities for the expansion of manufacture were great. The difficulties encountered were often of a twofold nature: lack of capital and lack of man power. We are here concerned only with the former.[14] If saving was for the purpose of investment, its form had to depend on the ability to serve this purpose. To expand industry required payment of wages, of royalties, and the purchase of raw materials. Most of these were as yet difficult to obtain on credit. It is not surprising, therefore, to find that saving became identified by most mercantilist writers with the storing of bullion. As to the way in which this storing of wealth was to be achieved, a whole host of proposals was offered. Predominant among these proposals was the advocacy of thrift and an export surplus. In the contemporary Puritan beliefs, thrift and saving were regarded as important virtues. Saving was, of course, stressed also with regard to expenditures, especially for wages. It is here that confusion arose for later interpreters of mercantilist doctrines. The fact that mercantilist writers not only condemned luxury consumption but also laid emphasis on the production of durable rather than consumable goods in general led modern writers to the conclusion that the mercantilists identified saving with durable goods as such.

[14] Wilson, *A Discourse upon Usury*, pp. 43 ff.

The important distinction to be made here is, however, that durable goods were tantamount to saving only if they were capable of furthering production. Only in so far as the durable goods were either so durable or so easily transportable and divisible that they could be used as means of exchange were they considered savings. The prime example here, of course, is the precious metals. The same reasoning applied when such goods were directly useful in the process of production, for example, in the form of raw materials. The latter question—the prohibition of the export of raw materials—was widely discussed by the mercantilists, but it would lead us too far afield to consider it here.

While the stress laid on the need for bullion for productive and derivatively for distributive purposes was based on a very real scarcity of the available means of exchange in relation to the economic needs, there were writers who tried to ridicule this insistence of their opponents on the need for remedying the existing scarcity of money. Jacob Viner quotes several of them, among them Thomas Mun. Interestingly enough, the quotation is taken from Mun's earlier tract, *Discourse of Trade,* which was written for the sole purpose of defending the East India Company against widespread attacks. It is perfectly true that the East India Company needed precious metals for their trade with the East Indies, but Mun is very careful to indicate that the real point is that this specie was spent for drugs and spices, which preserved health and cured disease, and on indigo and raw silk, which constituted necessary raw materials for the English manufactures.[15] Furthermore, Mun insisted that the East India Company exported, not English coins, but a limited amount of foreign coins.[16] And he continued to demonstrate that the re-export of the goods manufactured with the raw materials bought with the specie expended would bring in more specie than that originally laid out. It seems hardly justified to maintain that this

---

[15] *Cf.,* Thomas Mun, *Discourse of Trade from England unto the East Indies,* 1621, pp. 6–7, quoted by Johnson, in *Predecessors of Adam Smith,* p. 75.
[16] *Ibid.,* pp. 20, 31; also Feavearyear, *The Pound Sterling,* p. 139.

argument purports to show that there was actually no scarcity of money.[17]

One minor point can be made here in this connection. It may be said that there seems to be a contradiction in the mercantilists' doctrine advocating the export of manufactured goods, that is, frozen labor, for the purpose of acquiring larger amounts of bullion if the labor to be exported was itself scarce. The difference between bullion and labor, however, was that labor, while scarce at the moment, could be increased in various ways, and the mercantilists were busy in proposing not only practical measures, for example, the transformation of serfs and semi-serfs into manufacturing labor, but also various population theories including concrete suggestions for increasing the birth rate and decreasing the death rate.[18]

MERCANTILIST POLICIES WITH REGARD TO BULLION   If we want to summarize here some of the outstanding policies advocated by the mercantilists concerning bullion, we shall again have to fix our attention on the changing needs of the economic organism. Restrictions in the exportation of bullion were advocated long before the advent of the putting-out system or manufacturing production. The predominant reason at this earlier time was the maintenance of a war chest in order to hold—by force if necessary—a leading position as middle-man trader. "Pecunia nervus belli" was the reason for the accumulation of treasure, or as Trivulzio, Milanese *condottiere* answered, when asked what was most needed for war, "Three things must be ready: money, money, and once again, money." [19]

While the political requests for control of bullion exports were revised in the sixteenth century, recognition was gradually given to the fact that if bullion was needed for economic purposes it would be more efficient to regulate the flow of

[17] Cf. Viner, *Studies in the Theory of International Trade*, pp. 87–90.
[18] Sir William Petty, *Politicall Arithmitick*.
[19] Lodovico Guicciardini, *L'hore de recreatione*, in the German translation of Daniel Federmann von Memningen, Basel, 1575, quoted by Ehrenberg, in *Capital and Finance in the Age of the Renaissance*, p. 24.

precious metals by influencing the economic causes for this
flow rather than by the autocratic methods developed during
the formation of national states. Tawney and Power quote a
memorandum by an unidentified author in which it is stated
that "the straunger never respecteth our value, but the good-
ness of our coigne" and that therefore by a "reducement of
the monie greate numbres of her people might heavely
suffre." [20] The implication is that the normal change in the
value of money would not have the desired effect of providing
more money. Even inflation was proposed as a method to
attract foreign coin,[21] disregarding its effect upon the country
itself, to which the unknown author previously quoted had
referred. Again, it seems to us of little value to point out the
inconsistency in these two opinions. They are compatible if
related properly to the purposes which their writers had in
mind.

Direct methods were, however, still advocated as far as direct economic transactions were concerned. Generally accepted was the doctrine that high duties should be levied
upon most foreign imports. These duties were graduated according to the need for production at home, the highest duties
being placed on luxury goods. Export duties were generally
defended only when they were imposed upon raw materials
(particularly wool) which were needed for manufacture at
home. Export bounties, on the other hand, were generally
regarded favorably, and even the bounties granted in 1673
for the export of grain were not thought to constitute any
danger to the English home production. Only after 1750
writers begin to complain about the export bounty on grain,
because it kept the price of grain high at home and thus
tended to increase the price of labor or to make the latter dis-
contented and less efficient. The discussion on this point
grew to important proportions only after manufacturing pro-

[20] "Memorandum on the Reasons Moving Queen Elizabeth to Reform the
Coinage, 1559," in R. H. Tawney and E. Power, *Tudor Economic Documents*,
II, 194-95.
[21] Pauli, *Drei volkswirthschaftliche Denkschriften*, pp. 12 ff., quoted by
Viner, in *Studies in the Theory of International Trade*, p. 52.

duction had turned definitely into industrial production at the end of the eighteenth and beginning of the nineteenth century.

Closely connected with the problem of accumulating bullion for the purpose of expanding production was the argument for the protection of infant industries. Many times before and during this period the crown had been forced to take an active hand in the capitalization of new industries [22] because of the shortage of private capital and the relative abundance of credit. To be able to do this, the crown had to have capital at its disposal, and during this period that still meant, predominantly, hard money. The acceptance of the infant industry protection principle, which later was to play such an important part in international trade politics, was made possible during this time only in conjunction with the acquisition of bullion, since credit was not yet able to take its place. It is interesting that we meet this principle of infant industry protection as early as the seventeenth century in England and not, as we usually assume, only in the nineteenth century. The reason is that with respect to Flanders and Holland, England was at that time in a position similar to that in which Germany and the United States later found themselves in relation to England. The difference between the expostulation of this principle in the two different periods, as far as it is important to our problem, lies in the fact that in the earlier period the general conditions did not yet allow for expressing this principle in terms of economic equilibrium. The economic relations present a practical shortage in the supply of means of exchange as compared with the needs of production and distribution. The problem created by this deficiency, which so predominantly concerned the mercantilists, could be neglected by the classical economists because it had ceased to exist. In its place there appeared the static task, only now possible, of measuring the ideal proportional relations between volume of money and volume of commodities in terms of prices.

[22] For example, the tin industry of Cornwall.

THE FORMULATION OF THE QUANTITY THEORY OF MONEY   The development of the function of money has thus reached a stage in which the formulation of the new relation between the volume of money and volume of commodities became possible. Only in the later half of the eighteenth century had conditions advanced far enough to create those problems which are implied in what is generally known as the "quantity theory" of money. Malynes had already noticed an apparent direct relation between the volume of money and the prices of commodities. Pointing to the manipulation of exchange rates, he said that this

causeth . . . (as before) our monies to be transported and maketh scarcitie thereof, which abateth the price of our home commodities, and on the contrary advanceth the price of the forreine commodities beyond the seas, where our mony concurring with the monies of other countries causeth plenty, whereby the price of forrein commodities is advanced; and so might it fare with the price of our home commodities, being transported to those places, were we not hindred by the tolleration of their monies to go currant far above their value with them, and to the greater transportation of ours, and hinderance of importation of any unto us.[23]

John Locke discussed a still more advanced stage in the economic development when he maintained that there is a "Necessity of some Proportion of Money to Trade: But what Proportion that is, is hard to determine; because it depends not barely on the Quantity of Money, but the Quickness of its Circulation." By "money" he meant here not only as "Counters, for the Reckoning may be kept, or transferred by Writing; but on Money as a Pledge." He continued significantly that

Writing cannot supply the place of (money): Since the Bill, Bond, or other Note of Debt, I receive from one Man, will not be accepted as Security by another, he not knowing that the Bill or Bond is true or legal, or that the Man bound to me is honest or responsible; and so is not valuable enough to become a current Pledge, nor can by publick Authority be well made so, as in the

23 Malynes, reprinted in *Tudor Economic Documents* by R. H. Tawney, E. Power, p. 392.

Case of assigning of Bills. Because a Law cannot give to Bills that intrinsick Value, which the universal consent of Mankind has annexed to Silver and Gold. And hence Foreigners can never be brought to take your Bills, or Writings for any part of Payment, though perhaps they might pass as valuable Considerations among your own People, did not this very much hinder it, viz. That they are liable to unavoidable Doubt, Dispute, and Counterfeiting, and require other Proofs, to ussure us that they are true and good Security, than our Eyes or a Touchstone.[24]

This passage indicates well what we have been referring to previously, namely, that those means by which we have been accustomed to effectuate our economic transfers for the last 130 years had not yet developed far enough to serve that purpose up to the time of Locke. The relation between money and prices is understood by Locke in the following way:

to keep your Trade going without Loss, your Commodities amongst you must keep an equal, or, at least, near the Price of the same Species of Commodities in the neighboring Countries: which they cannot do, if your Money be far less than in other Countries; for then, either your Commodities must be sold very cheap, or a great Part of your Trade must stand still, there not being Money enough in the Country to pay for them (in their shifting of Hands) at that high Price, which the Plenty, and consequently low Value of Money makes them at in another Country. For the Value of Money in general is the Quantity of all the Money in the World, in Proportion to all the Trade: But the Value of Money in any one Country, is the present Quantity of the current Money in that Country, in Proportion to the present Trade.[25]

It may be well at this point to recall a few dates in the monetary history of England. The precious metals in circulation were badly clipped, by the King as well as by the goldsmiths. The need of the Crown for money and the high interest which the latter was willing to pay had made it possible for the goldsmiths to lend money, that is, precious metals, to the Crown which they themselves had previously taken into safekeeping from the various merchants.[26] In 1666 an act was passed which abolished the mint charges, encouraging thus

[24] Locke, *The Works,* p. 12.   [25] *Ibid.,* p. 24.
[26] An excellent account of this process is given in Feavearyear, *The Pound Sterling,* pp. 91 ff.

the coinage of silver. But in spite of the relative success of this act, the shortage of money persisted, and the price of silver rose steadily until the recoinage in 1696. Gradually during this time bills came into existence for use in the internal trade, mainly for the reason of avoiding risky transportation. These bills, however, did not yet increase the available volume of means of exchange "any more than a postal order (does) today." [27]

The first institutional basis on a larger scale for "artificially" increasing the volume of currency by means of paper money was provided by the passage of the Tonnage Act of 1694, by which the Bank of England was established. On the basis of this Act, the Bank was permitted to issue bills up to the amount of its original capital of 1.2 million pounds sterling. The amount of 720 thousand pounds had been used for rediscount of Tallies,[28] and as soon as the remaining 480 thousand pounds were issued the Court of Directors of the Bank of England decided to issue over and above the authorized amount: cashier notes, the so-called Speed's notes, signed only with the name of the cashier, from which these notes received their name. Most of this took place after John Locke had written his famous essay on money.

To these facts another must be added. The trade of the East India Company really began to flourish after the Restoration, and with it a loophole was opened through which England's silver was increasingly drained. When in 1717 this company transferred three million ounces of silver,[29] one of the results of this drain was an increasing shortage of the

[27] *Ibid.*, p. 91.

[28] Tallies were an ancient form of receipts or vouchers. A piece of wood shaped like a thick knife blade was notched at the edges to show the amount of money or goods changing hands. Notches of different sizes represented the different denominations of money or weight. The nature of transaction was then written in duplicate on the two sides. The piece of wood was split lengthwise through the notches by means of a cut parallel to the sides. Each party kept a part, a thin piece of notched wood with writing on one side. If either party disputed the payment, the matter could easily be settled by fixing the two parts together to see whether or not they matched. Tallies were used in the exchequer until 1827 (*Dictionary of Political Economy*, ed. by Sir Robert Palgrave, pp. 513–514).

[29] Lord Stanhope in the House of Lords, January 3, 1719, quoted by Feavearyear, *The Pound Sterling*, p. 142.

smaller units of the means of exchange and a consequent increased outcry for some remedy. At the same time, however,
this outflow of silver helped to eliminate gradually a source
of currency disturbance by lessening the importance of the
ratio between silver and gold.[30] This development led without any conscious intention to the *de facto* establishment of
a gold standard in England in the first half of the eighteenth
century.

These changes go a long way toward explaining the difference between the approaches of John Locke and David Hume
to monetary problems. Hume's most important work in this
field, *The Political Discourses,* was published in 1752, a few
years before the establishment of country banking in England,
which later finally succeeded in alleviating the scarcity of
means of exchange for the smaller producer. Industrial production, however, with its attendant increasing importance
of wage payments, did not develop to pre-eminent national importance until the latter half of the eighteenth century. We
must keep these points in mind in the following discussion
of Hume's first classical statement of the quantity theory of
money. We should remember that the flow of money with
which he was primarily concerned was still directed by the
big merchants of the manufacturing period, who were merchants and interested in manufacture at the same time. The
institutional division between trade and production developed only in a later period.

THE QUANTITATIVE RELATION OF MONEY AND PRICES   Hume
starts his discussion on the effects of changes in the volume
of money with the statement:

All augmentation has no other effect than to heighten the price of
labor and commodities; and even this variation is little more than
that of a name. In the progress towards these changes, the augmentation may have some influence, by exciting industry; but
after the prices are settled, suitably to the new abundance of gold
and silver, it has no manner of influence.[31]

[30] See p. 9.
[31] Hume, *Political Discourses,* reprinted in Monroe, *Early Economic
Thought,* pp. 311–312.

Elsewhere he says:

If we consider any one kingdom by itself, it is evident, that the greater or less plenty of money is of no consequence; since the prices of commodities are always proportioned to the plenty of money.[32]

These views of Hume are important since their verity is demonstrable in contemporary reality. It is now interesting to observe how Hume projects the structure of his contemporary reality back into the past, an excellent example of rationalizing an assumedly historical deduction *ex post facto*. He notices that there were and that there still are "some kingdoms and many provinces in Europe (and all of them were once in the same condition), where money is so scarce, that the landlord can get none at all from his tenants; but is obliged to take his rent in kind." [33] But what happens if money begins to stream into the country?

Some time is required before the money circulates through the whole state, and makes its effect be felt on all ranks of people. At first, no alteration is perceived; by degrees the price rises, first of one commodity, then of another; till the whole at last reaches a just proportion with the new quantity of specie which is in the kingdom. In my opinion, it is only in this interval or intermediate situation, between the acquisition of money and rise of prices, that the encreasing quantity of gold and silver is favourable to industry. When any quantity of money is imported into a nation, it is not at first dispersed into many hands; but is confined to the coffers of a few persons, who immediately seek to employ it to advantage. Here are a set of manufacturers or merchants, we shall suppose, who have received returns of gold and silver for goods which they sent to Cadiz. They are thereby enabled to employ more workmen than formerly, who never dream of demanding higher wages, but are glad of employment from such good paymasters. If workmen become scarce, the manufacturer gives higher wages, but at first requires an increase of labour; and this is willingly submitted to by the artisan, who can now eat and drink better, to compensate his additional toil and fatigue. He carries his money to market, where he finds every thing at the same price as formerly, but he returns with greater quantity and of better kinds, for the use of his family. The farmer and gardener, finding, that all their com-

[32] Hume, *Essays, Moral, Political and Literary*, p. 309.   [33] *Ibid.*, p. 315.

modities are taken off, apply themselves with alacrity to the raising more; and at the same time can afford to take better and more
cloths from their tradesmen, whose price is the same as formerly,
and their industry only whetted by so much new gain.[34]

What Hume is describing here is his own time. He mis-
takes it, however, as our historians and theorists have been
inclined to mistake it ever since, for the historical development which had led up to these times,[35] There is an essential
difference between a part of society which is developing a
new mode of production and one which, after this new mode
of production has been developed elsewhere, tries to bridge
the gap and to reach immediately the developed level. The
process of bridging the gap will differ materially from that of
creating a new type of production. When England developed
large-scale manufacturing on the basis of free labor, it had
to create at the same time those institutions which Hume did
not consider any longer "the wheels of trade." To him they
had become "the oil which renders the motion of the wheels

[34] *Ibid.*, pp. 313–314.

[35] He follows the same procedure in his tract on interest. When he begins
to explain "the causes and the effects of a great or small demand for borrowing," he says that "When a people have emerged ever so little from a savage
state, and their numbers have encreased beyond the original multitude,
there must immediately arise an inequality of property; and while some
possess large tracts of land, others are confined within narrow limits, and
some are entirely without any landed property. Those who possess more
land than they can labour, employ those who possess none, and agree to
receive a determinate part of the product. Thus the landed interest is immediately established; nor is there any settled government, however rude, in
which affairs are not on this footing. Of these proprietors of land, some must
presently discover themselves to be of different tempers from others; and
while one would willingly store up the produce of his land for futurity, another desires to consume at present what would suffice for many years." "In
a state, therefore, where there is nothing but a landed interest, as there is
little frugality, the borrowers must be very numerous, and the rate of interest
must hold proportion to it" (pp. 322–323). He adds seemingly correctly that
"The difference depends not on the quantity of money, but on the habits
and manners which prevail." The habits and manners are determined by the
specific stage to which the mode of production has developed, and the concrete institutions of that stage will to some extent depend on facilities that
may have been created elsewhere at an earlier date. This especially is relevant to the development of so-called "late" countries or of colonial countries.
Both of the latter find to a certain extent the institution of credit ready-
made for them by previously developed industrial countries, and to them
scarcity of money or capital must have a different meaning.

more smooth and easy." [36] That was perfectly true for his time, but it was never true for the time which we have been discussing in our earlier chapters. Here, again, we can observe the urgent necessity of always reminding ourselves of the concrete contents of the terms which we are using. We were careful to point out that in the early manufacturing period, money, *de facto,* was identical with bullion, and we showed later on how this form of money gradually changed its character through the development of credit and the eventually possible use of fiduciary money. Hume identifies semantically, as has so often been done, the historical contents of the term "money" and its "form" in the early manufacturing period with its function during the late manufacturing and early industrial period because of the merely formal identity of terms. He constructed for himself an imaginary history of economic development, just as the different nations today construct their political histories. Only in this way could Hume come to his conclusion for earlier times as well as his own: "From the whole of this reasoning . . . that it is no manner of consequence with regard to the domestic happiness of a state, whether money be in a greater or less quantity." [37] Only after the period of manufacture had fully developed was it possible for money to react directly on prices to any important extent. Before this stage was actually reached the commercial and even more so the productive relations were not yet integrated and regularized enough. Under these conditions the actual function of the means of exchange simply could not be the same as it became after the integration of production and distribution and after the introduction of more adequate means of communication and transportation. When this development had become strong enough to be visible, Hume made the most penetrating observations of the functioning of the means of exchange under the new conditions. Economic society, as it then came into being, did allow for the beginning of a banking system, for credit among well-established merchant houses, and for pub-

---

[36] Hume, *Essays, Moral, Political and Literary,* p. 309.   [37] *Ibid.,* p. 315.

lic credit of a government—in all of which continuity and
interdependence were no longer questioned. Thus, to Hume
the main problem became the effect produced by the quantitative variations of the available means of exchange in relation to the volume of commodities in transaction. There
existed an amount of money at any one time adequate for
the volume of commodity exchanges transacted, not more
and not less. Hume was primarily concerned with the possible result of a greater or smaller quantity either of money
in relation to commodities or of commodities in relation to
money, as such variations became noticeable within the whole
economic structure.

We have quoted Hume as saying that any increase or decrease in the amount of precious metals and as a matter of fact
any increase or decrease in the amount of money "is of no
consequence . . . if we consider any one kingdom by itself." [38] He should have added: "at any given time." The
latter he actually implied when he discussed in detail the
events which were likely to take place after the volume
of money had increased. He comes to the conclusion that
nothing has altered in the relation of money and commodities.

In elaborating and in going to the particulars of his basic
views Hume laid bare much of that monetary mechanism
which is so often assumed today to have prevailed for the 150
years following the publication of his *Discourse*. Hume observed that "the prices do not so much depend on the absolute
quantity of commodities and then of money, which are in a
nation, as on that of the commodities which come or may
come to market and of the money which circulates." [39] Hence,
Hume does not limit the conditions of circulation to money
alone, but extends it to commodities, "as money and commodities . . . never meet, they cannot affect each other." [40]
The volume of commodities may be increasing, and such an
increase would neutralize an increase in the volume of money,
with the result that the prices either would remain equal or

---

[38] *Ibid.*, p. 309.   [39] *Ibid.*, p. 316.   [40] *Ibid.*, pp. 316, 317.

would not increase in proportion to the absolute increase in the volume of money.

We have now collected most of the elements of the flow of money in the middle of the eighteenth century as Hume presented them. The outstanding characteristic of his theory is that money and prices find themselves in an equational relationship. If the volume of the effective means of exchange increases while the volume of commodities in transaction remain stable, the prices of these commodities must increase, and *vice versa*. The logical, as well as the theoretical, basic assumption in this formulation is that this is so because there are no disturbing factors in the process of production, and any changes in the volume of means of exchange can have only temporary effects. It may be mentioned parenthetically that Hume has recognized that "a nation, whose money decreases, is actually, at that time, weaker and more miserable than another nation, which possesses no more money, but is on the encreasing hand." This occurs only temporarily, because the changes in the volume of money "are not immediately attended with proportionable alterations in the prices of commodities." [41] But at the same time Hume emphasized that "the want of money can never injure any state within itself: For men and commodities are the real strength of any community." [42] We then find here that there is still one essential element lacking in Hume's theory if we compare his theory with the nineteenth century quantity theory of money. He does not assume an absolute reciprocal relationship between the two sides of the equation. He is still convinced that "money is nothing but the representation of labour and commodities, and serves only as a method of rating or estimating them." [43]

The mercantilist notion that money—in their case bullion —could be one of the main incentives for investment was entirely lacking in Hume's theory. This was quite correct, because money (bullion) was a condition for investment only as long as it was scarce, for reasons which we have outlined

[41] *Ibid.,* p. 315.   [42] *Ibid.,* p. 319.   [43] *Ibid.,* p. 312.

above. These reasons had disappeared at the time of Hume. We might add that to some extent there is implicit in Hume's insistence upon the predominant importance of production a more modern version of economic theory which maintains that economic production will run smoothly irrespective of any influence from purely monetary sources as long as production itself does not exhibit any structural mutations; if it does exhibit such changes, no monetary manipulations will be able to do away with them. This is somewhat similar to Hume's contention that no augmentation or decrease in the volume of money could make any lasting difference to production. We will discuss this point in detail below.

Concluding our investigation into Hume's quantity theory of money, we may say that Hume's formulation appears on the surface to imply an *equilibrium principle,* inasmuch as he maintains that any change on whatever side of the equation will result in the arrival at a new equilibrium. We have noticed, however, that to Hume money is still a function of production. Naturally enough, he took the particular nature of the productive process of his time for granted, projecting it simply not only backwards as we have pointed out above but also forward in order to be able to assume static conditions. He saw for the later development further increases in the volume of production, but he did not, and as a matter of fact could not, foresee the gradual emergence of generic change within the still very young industrial production. Only after the structural change had become visible at a much later period were these tendencies to be formulated into the laws of the *dynamics* of industrial society as distinct from the *mechanics* with which Hume was concerned.

Part II · *The Formulation of the Classical Quantity Theory*

5 · The Issues in the Bullion Controversy

HISTORICAL BACKGROUND   By the end of the eighteenth century the industrial type of production of commodities had become prevalent, bringing in its wake a development of regular interrelationships between the various producers and consumers. Adam Smith, in his discussion of the division of labor, has given an adequate picture of that society.

There is little doubt that the theory of money would have retained its position of secondary importance in the general economic theory of that period if it had not been for the occurrence of particularly striking events which forced the political and economic strategists to concern themselves particularly with disentangling the apparently highly important flux of money. One extraordinary event was the French Revolution, which to the English merchant produced an economic-political threat of first importance.

It might seem hard to understand why the English merchants were ready to exhaust their last economic and financial resources to combat this Revolution, since it seemed to bring about in France only the same social conditions of economic and political democracy of which the English were so proud. What, then, was it that induced the merchants of England to fight the French Revolution? First of all, let us remember that not all industrial development in France had been oppressed before the Revolution. Luxury goods production, as a matter of fact, had not only been permitted, but had been subsidized. This had been of little concern to the English, inasmuch as they themselves were not competitors in this line of production. Now, after the Revolution, that type of industry in which England was engaged, which today we would be tempted to call large-scale industry with mass production of products, became possible in France. Its political and economic suppression had disappeared with the disappearance of the *Ancien Régime*. In other words, the French Revolution did loose forces which were to threaten actively the English supremacy in the foreign markets.

Secondly, and perhaps more important, the French Revolution was by no means only a liberation of the *bourgeoisie*. Once the political transformation was under way, it became apparent that large social forces were threatening to maintain a supremacy, forces that were liked neither by the French *bourgeoisie* nor by the English. The lower classes, the workers, craftsmen, and peasants, as well as a small part of the intelligentsia, all of whom had been called to aid the French *bourgeoisie* in its struggle against the political might of the *Ancien Régime,* announced their own political and economic counter-demands, and it was readily seen that their concept of *Liberté, Egalité, Fraternité* was at variance with that of the *bourgeoisie*. In the midst of the bourgeois revolution the *bourgeoisie* therefore made a complete turn, and like the famous Scarlet Pimpernel, allied itself with those reactionary forces which it just previously had started out to combat. The role of the English in this social process was full of meaning if we remember the old Caesarian principle of *divide et impera*. The French *bourgeoisie* were combatted in the first stage of the Revolution as potential competitors, and in the later stage were aided, in fear of the plebeian masses at home. The result of this historically necessary attitude was the series of Anglo-French wars, in the monetary consequences of which we are interested.

There was, then, a definite connection between the Revolution in France and conditions in England. At that time England was expanding industrially at an enormous rate, but it was just this rate of industrial progress which created in England severe difficulties, in the light of which the French Revolution and its threat to established institutions assumed the form of an internal danger.

In the treatises on money, concerned with the doctrines elaborated in this period, it has always been emphasized that the military expenditures during this time were of an *extraordinary* nature. The difficulties which arose out of the structural transformation which took place in England quite irrespective of the foreign wars are curiously neglected. It is, of course, perfectly true that one cannot distinguish clearly and in absolute terms between "indigenous" development and "influences from the outside." It amounts to a tautology, today, to say that the causes of the French Revolution and the reasons for its being disliked by the English merchants were part and parcel of the same economic phenomena by which industrial society in England developed. At the same time, it is important to point out that England itself was shaken by one of the most important revolutions in human history. The tremendous increase in productive capacity, the increase in population, the disproportionality between income and output arising from the persistence of the Corn Laws, was leading in England to a political situation which in many respects approximated the radicalism produced in the United States, as well as in France. Strikes, bread riots, and machine wrecking swept over the country, and soldiers were frequently used to suppress disorders. In 1794 Pitt suspended habeas corpus for eight years.

This historical development led to revolutions in America and France, but not in England. The important difference between the development in England and that in the remaining countries was that England had begun to tap the enormous potential economic wealth accessible through the industrial mode of production. England had at that time this key to the temporary solution of the difficulties already in its hands. The other nations had still to engage in the creation of the basis upon which such production was possible, a stage England had passed in the preceding years. On the other side, the very existence in England of industrial production tended to increase the social contradictions in the remaining countries and to a degree which turned social transformations into social revolutions.

THE MONETARY ISSUES   Hume had presented a picture of society in which there was possible a perfect harmony between money and prices as long as there were no artificial interferences on the monetary side of the equation and as long as on the commodity side the English producers continued to make strides such as those for which they were being eulogized by their contemporaries. Into this harmony the political events described in the introductory paragraphs came as a terrific shock. To wage wars means to support armies, and it proved to be an important point for the development of monetary theory at that time that these armies were operating outside England. We must add here that by "armies" we do not mean only the English armies operating in France, Holland, and Belgium, but also the German, Austrian, Italian, Sicilian armies operating against France. The direct loans made by England, according to Silberling,[1] ran into several millions of English pounds. The amount nearly reached the staggering sum of 60 million pounds.[2] In the same table by Silberling we also find figures covering the expenditures for the British armies in Europe. These payments to foreign countries were in many respects similar to the credits that were made available to Poland, Rumania, Greece, and Turkey by Mr. Chamberlain in 1939. Professor Silberling has also made extensive investigations of the actual physical transfers of the earlier time.[3] The volume of the extraordinary remittances is thus approximately known, also the source of these remittances.[4]

Why had the premium for precious metals risen above par?

[1] Silberling, "Financial and Monetary Policy of Great Britain during the Napoleonic Wars," *Quarterly Journal of Economics*, XXXVIII, 225.

[2] *Ibid.*, p. 227.

[3] *Ibid.*, pp. 214–233; also, Silberling, "British Prices and Business Cycles," *Review of Economic Statistics*, Supplement No. 2, October, 1923, pp. 233–261.

[4] Silberling, "British Financial Policy," *Review of Economic Statistics*, p. 217.

This question was of major importance to English foreign trade for several reasons. In the first place, it made foreign goods more expensive in England at a time when large imports were of primary importance to the country because of the war situation and the generally increasing needs for supplementary food stuffs on account of bad harvests. Furthermore, England's trade with India was based on large exports of silver, and its acquisition now proved to be more expensive. It is therefore a rather curious position in which the leading English financiers found themselves during this time. On the one hand, there was no question about the necessity of carrying on the war against the French, and little opposition appeared, therefore, against the need of the government for large loans or increased taxes, as long as the latter was predominantly indirect taxation, which would be least burdensome for the financiers. But while all this was true, they were considerably put out when this war finance began to be accompanied by a premium on precious metals over the English paper currency.

The premium appeared first in 1795, one year before the Restriction Act. It increased with the passage of the Restriction Act, but decreased immediately thereafter, making possible a negative premium or unfavorable rate differential in 1798,[5] and then reappeared in 1799. There seem to have been few comments on the government's monetary policy before Boyd's letter to Pitt in 1801. This letter initiated, however, a whole flood of controversial literature. Two more-or-less distinct positions became observable. On the one side were those who attacked the government for allowing the occurrence of the premium of precious metals over the now-existing paper

---

[5] The following is an interesting comment as far as the provinces were concerned: "Dr. James Currie writes, under the date of February 22, 1797: 'Orders have been sent up to London to sell [funds] without restriction to a great amount. . . . A principal banker told me that money had flowed back on him so much that he was absolutely at a loss what to do with it; as he, for his own part, would not purchase another sixpence in the funds, and could not lend it out on commercial adventure in the present state of things. Thus large sums are beginning to rest in the bankers' hands without the power of converting them into account'" (Hughes, *Liverpool Banks and Bankers*, p. 17).

money and proposed the explanation that the abandonment of the metallic standard and the establishment of the premium were cause and effect. The remedy this group proposed, therefore, was to return to the metallic standard. They were, accordingly, named "bullionists." Those defending the government and its monetary policy were labeled "antibullionists."

6 · The Theory of Inflation

POSITIONS ON THE BULLIONIST THEORIES   Boyd, in his letter to Pitt, said that "the premium of bullion, the low rate of exchange, and the high prices of commodities in general [are to be regarded as] . . . symptoms and effects of the superabundance of paper." [1] Thornton argued similarly in his *Paper Credit*.[2] He elaborated the results of an increase in the volume of currency and showed that such an increase must necessarily lead to higher prices at home as well as to a premium on bullion.

Bullion is a commodity . . . and it rises and falls in value on the same principle as all other commodities. It becomes, like them, dear in proportion as the circulating medium is rendered dear.[3]

From this it follows that

there arises that temptation . . . either to convert back into bullion and then to export; or, which is the same thing, to export and convert back into bullion, and then sell to the bank, at the price which would be gained by exportation, that gold which the bank has purchased, and has converted from bullion into coin. In this manner an increase of paper . . . contributes to produce an excess of the market price above the mint price of gold and to prevent, therefore, the introduction of a proper supply of it into the Bank of England.[4]

Thornton argues extensively against Adam Smith, whom he blames for having explained a possible premium of bullion over the mint price exclusively as "something in the state of the coin." [5] Thornton makes, however, a second and more important attack against Adam Smith's theory of international exchange. Adam Smith had pointed out that in the case of an excess issue, paper would be changed into coin and coin be exported. Thornton shows that every increase in paper

---

[1] Boyd, *Letter to . . . Pitt*, 2d ed., p. xxxi.
[2] Henry Thornton, *An Enquiry into the Nature and Effects of the Paper Credit of Great Britain*, especially chap. viii, pp. 192 ff.
[3] *Ibid.*, p. 202.   [4] *Ibid.*, p. 203.
[5] *Ibid.*, p. 205; Smith, *The Wealth of Nations*, 4th ed., I, 69; I, 451; Vol. II, Book IV, chap. vi, pp. 333–335.

would increase the price of goods, "which advanced price of goods affords employment to a larger quantity of circulating medium, so that the circulation can never be said to be over full." On the basis of this statement, Thornton makes the inference that from Smith's explanation we are led to believe that "the expense of restoring it consists merely in the charge of collecting it and transporting it from the place to which it is gone." [6] He points out that aside from the expenses, the gold may have to be purchased

at a loss, and at a loss which may be either more or less considerable; a circumstance of great importance in the question. If this loss should ever become extremely great, the difficulties of restoring the value of our paper might not easily be surmounted, and a current discount or difference between the coin and paper of the country would scarcely be avoidable. [7]

Thornton, however, does not say that Smith was proposing an advisable policy for a bank *within a country*. Smith did not argue this case on an international basis because at his time few problems, if any, of this type were found in the *international* monetary relations. Thornton is unaware of the fact that he argues the point of an excess issue as it occurred at his time and that the conditions which led to this excess were by no means as general and valid for all times as he presupposed. [8] We find it difficult to pronounce judgment in the manner of previous investigators of this period, but, rather, feel constrained to say that every one of the writers was concerned with problems *of his time* and in consequence had to be at variance with the pronouncements of earlier writers, who had been occupied with their problems. If we wish to distinguish between right and wrong explanations, we have to refer either to contemporaneous writers who hold different opinions upon the same subject matter at the same time, or

[6] Thornton, *An Enquiry into the Nature and Effects of the Paper Credit of Great Britain,* pp. 211–212.

[7] *Ibid.,* pp. 211–212.

[8] Ricardo has made somewhat similar comment on Thornton's argument (Ricardo, "High Price of Bullion," in his *Works,* p. 277).

we must account for the economic structural changes which have taken place meanwhile.

To come back to Thornton, he makes it quite clear that in his analysis he is concerned with the maintenance of a certain value of money and with "the difficulties of restoring the value of our paper." That, however, was decidedly not the interest of Adam Smith. He was primarily interested in the preservation of an adequate relation between prices and commodities. Thornton used this reasoning to argue a special case, namely, the restoration of the currency to that value which, for reasons indicated below, was of important advantage to him and his group. To put it in still other words, Thornton presupposed a desirable value of money, the achieving of which he considered the primary task of the directors of the Bank of England.

It is at this point that we wish to point out a basic difference in the approach to the explanation of the flux of money in this period as compared to the preceding one. It seems interesting that Thornton and his fellow bullionists, aside from occasional vague remarks, do not seem to have indicated any interest in the fact that the volume of production at that time was increasing considerably. Adam Smith and Hume had been very conscious of this fact. Is it possible to discover in the economic events which had taken place meanwhile a sufficient reason for this, at least temporary, neglect on the part of the bullionist school?

From a somewhat different angle we may call attention to the fact that most, if not all, of the bullionists were London merchants, and as such were primarily interested in foreign trade relations rather than domestic production, and that their commercial activity was intimately bound up with the price of silver. We may add that a similar attitude of these merchants can be observed in connection with the evaluation of the function of the country banks. Thornton treats this function in a very peculiar way. At no place does he elaborate on their role of providing an expanding productive society with the necessary capital for such an expansion. All he does is to use them as an analogy to international monetary relations and in so doing to expose them as the places in which speculative credit originated. It is not intended to offer here an *advocatio diabolica* for the country banks. Any rapid process of expansion, however, will be accompanied necessarily by speculative characteristics. But it goes much too far to center one's attention *only* on this feature in discussing the country banks. It affords no difficulty to Thornton to assume that any willingness on the side of the country banks to extend credit will be met with an adequate demand for such credit. The important thing, however, would be to point out the reasons why, in spite of the deplored condition of the currency, there was such a widespread optimism in the circles of the producers, because it was, after all, primarily the producers whom the country banks served. Since production was expanding and, as can be shown, expanding at a rapid rate, it is difficult to see how the expansion of credit by the country banks could lead to an inflationary increase in prices.

Not least important is, finally, the development of new economic interest, that of the long-term industrial creditor. The importance of the gradual development of credit, in the form of deferring payments as well as of silent investments, cannot be underestimated. An interest in the maintenance of a certain value of money has to come about at the moment in which the value of those contracts is endangered by rising prices. It is of secondary importance in this connection whether these rising prices were brought about by the occasion of large extraordinary expenditures, as, for instance, for war purposes, or as temporary discrepancies accompanying a rapid though intermittent expansion in the volume of production once this production has been established as an integrated part of social life. It seems to us that we now have the clue to the attitude of the first quantity theorists and to their neglect of one of the possible grave implications of price changes.

To return to the problem of explaining the premium paid for precious metals over the mint prices and to elucidate its consequences, Thornton pointed out that a premium occasioned by a prolonged excess issue had necessarily to be abortive. The Bank would have to try to buy gold at the advanced price to be able to meet the demands for gold through the presentation of its notes. This gold would be melted by those who had obtained it, and after being melted would be bought by the Bank in order to be coined into guineas. If the Bank carries on "this sort of contest with the melters, [it] is obviously waging a very unequal war; and even though it should not be tired early, it will be likely to be tired sooner than its adversaries." [9] Or in Ricardo's words, "The Bank would be obliged, therefore, ultimately, to adopt the only remedy in their power to put a stop to the demand for guineas." [10] Ricardo argued on much the same grounds as Thornton correcting here and there some minor misconceptions of Thornton. He came to the well-known conclusion that the two tests to be applied in the determination of an excess issue are absolutely valid, namely, the status of the exchange quotation of the English currency with other countries and the price of bullion. He held that because of the influence of the exchange rates on the flow of commodities and the demand for bullion, any continuous unfavorable exchange could be called only a depreciation of currency. While Thornton, in 1802, was still in a position to leave the way open to explain the unfavorable exchange by an unfavorable balance of trade, Ricardo points out that the limit for the effects of an unfavorable balance "is probably 4 or 5 percent. This will not account for a depreciation of 15 or 20 percent." [11] According to the principles which Thornton and Ricardo held in common, this unfavorable exchange "is to be accounted for only by the depreciation of the circulating medium." [12] The remedy which Ricardo proposed was the removal of the restriction against gold payments by the Bank of England. "If the Bank were to diminish the quantity of their notes until they had increased their value 15

[9] Thornton, *An Enquiry into . . . Paper Credit,* p. 125.
[10] *Cf.,* Ricardo, "High Price of Bullion," in his *Works,* p. 267.
[11] *Ibid.,* p. 280.   [12] *Ibid.,* p. 281.

percent, the restriction might be safely removed, as there would then be no temptation to export specie." [13]

The main argument, then, of the bullionist position seems to be that a return to a metallic standard would offer the only means to measure the volume of currency in circulation in relation to the volume of commodities to be exchanged. The implications in this statement will be discussed after we have briefly presented the opinions of the so-called antibullionists.

It is to be remembered that we are interested here, not primarily in recounting old controversies, but in the detection of the process of doctrine formation and its relation to the problems in economic reality with which these doctrines were concerned. It is therefore of little importance to follow every individual deviation in these controversies, especially if the arguments relate directly to the personal economic position which its advocates maintained.

Most antibullionists were in one way or another connected with the government, and in many of the discussions the need for a defense for the measures taken by the government became apparent. Thus, for instance, the proof offered by means of available statistics that the volume of the notes of the Bank of England had not increased and that there was no necessary connection between the differing volumes of paper currency and the fluctuations of the exchange rates or the bullion quotations was easily refuted by Ricardo, who said

that whilst the high price of bullion and the low exchange rates continue, and whilst our gold is undebased, it would to me be no proof of our currency not being depreciated if there were only 5 millions of bank notes in circulation. When we speak, therefore, of an excess of bank notes, we mean that portion of the amount of the issues of the Bank which can now circulate, but could not, if the currency were of its bullion value. When we speak of an excess of country currency, we mean a portion of the amount of the country bank notes which cannot be absorbed in the circulation because they are exchangeable for, and are depreciated below, the value of bank notes.[14]

[13] *Ibid.*, p. 279.
[14] Ricardo, "Reply to Mr. Bosanquet," in his *Works*, pp. 349–350.

Professor Viner recently raised the point, in discussing the bullionist position, that "throughout the controversy . . . bank deposits [were] . . . either overlooked or else held not to be currency." [15] Samuel Turner once defined a country bank as

a kind of clearing house, where, without any actual interchange of notes or money, the greater part of all payments between man and man was effectuated by mere transfers in the books of their bankers. . . . It was merely the smaller payments for wages and weekly bills which required notes.[16]

Another point raised by the antibullionists was that in times of large-scale monetary remittances and heavy purchasing of corn because of increased needs of the army, as well as because of bad harvests at home, the balance of exchange operations had to be disturbed, and that it was this tendency toward an unfavorable balance which forced the rate of exchange for that time below par.[17] Ricardo maintained at first that whatever the reasons for the unfavorable status of the exchange rates, the exchange rates would adjust themselves automatically to the previous level.[18] He was supported in this contention by Wheatley, who even more rigidly contended that

when the equilibrium of money is . . . altered between any two nations . . . it is natural for the person who trades in bullion, like the merchant who trades in any other commodity, to profit by this variation, export his merchandise where it will fall to most advantage . . . the instant the equilibrium is avowedly affected by the volume of exchange, it becomes his interest to transmit it from the country where it is cheaper to the country where it is dearest, in order to receive his profit.[19]

This apparently highly controversial point seems, however, to be on a verbal level if we consider realistically the circum-

[15] Viner, *Studies in the Theory of International Trade*, p. 130.

[16] Turner, *Considerations upon the Agriculture, Commerce and Manufactures of the British Empire*, pp. 54–55.

[17] Boase, "A Letter to . . . Lord King in Defense of the Conduct of the Directors of the Bank of England and Ireland," pp. 22–23.

[18] Ricardo, "Reply to Mr. Bosanquet," in his *Works*, p. 56.

[19] Wheatley, *Remarks on Currency and Commerce*, p. 56.

stances involved. If only occasional remittances had been made to foreign countries, there seems little doubt that Ricardo's prediction of a rather speedy adjustment would have been true. Actually, however, the remittances were continuous and left during the duration of a war little possibility for the predicted adjustments to operate. Many of Ricardo's fellow bullionists conceded this point, and it seems that Ricardo himself, when confronted with the direct question and not with a statement of general principles, actually approached this point of view very closely.[20] On the other side, the antibullionists readily conceded that the adjustment predicted by the bullionists would take place soon after the removal of the cause for the disturbances, that is, the cause for lowering the exchange rates, which in this case had been the forced expenditures abroad for the war.

Ricardo's endlessly repeated solution to the existing difficulties was curtailment of the volume of currency. "Diminish the currency by calling in the excess of Bank notes . . . and what can prevent . . . an importation of gold and consequently a favourable exchange?"[21] The antibullionists, as far as they were representatives of the government, denied the advisability of such a policy under the existing conditions of war. The so-called antibullionists of the Bank of England type had, however, quite different reasons for being interested at least in the temporary maintenance of the existing volume of paper. It is true that the Bank of England had been established by London merchants. The successors of these London merchants were still largely engaged in overseas trade. The Bank itself, however, established with the purpose of making profits and gaining the privilege of continuing to make profits, but under the cloak of aid to the government, had become with time less

[20] Ricardo, Appendix to "Reply to Mr. Bosanquet," p. 363, where he denies awareness "of any causes but excess . . . which could produce such effects as we have for a *considerable time* witnessed," admitting therewith and stating at another place (p. 364) that he is not disposed "to contend that the issues of one day, or of one month, can produce any effect on the foreign exchanges; it may possibly require a period of more permanent duration; an interval is absolutely necessary before such effects would follow."

[21] *The Morning Chronicle,* September 14, 1809.

wedded to the particular interests of its one-time founders and began to lean toward the new sources of profits which had for some time been developing in England. These sources involved the expansion of English productive enterprise. Long enough had the Bank of England refused to accommodate those country merchants who had turned producer, as well as the newly developed type of the industrial entrepreneur. Cold-shouldered by the Old Lady of Threadneedle Street, they had begun to develop effectively their own institutions. Now, under the conditions of the commercial war, industry was not only expanding but was also offered ample opportunities for speculative excesses. And in these golden opportunities the Bank of England wanted to partake. We thus see the directors of the Bank of England under the guise of theoretical advocacy of antibullionist doctrines busily engaged in defending the abundance of available money, which they were equally busily engaged in lending out.

Admittedly, it is difficult to disentangle today the principal use to which those commercial credits were put, but from indirect evidence it can be assumed that they were used for productive and speculative purposes within the country rather than as formerly in international trade. This suggestion seems even more likely when we consider that during the time of the commercial wars and after the loss of the American colonies the overseas trade tended to revert to the west coast of England, thereby giving rise to new large banking establishments like Gurney, Hoare and Harman, who financed the trade between Liverpool and Philadelphia by means of Quaker bills and linked their transactions with Hamburg. At the same time, Ireland and Scotland offered accommodations to the country banks of Manchester and Lancashire. In the bullion controversy we can thus observe a more amiable phase of the struggle between bullion and bills, that period in which the Bank of England still tried to participate more or less peacefully in the profits coming from the new trade. In contrast, we find later, in the forty years after 1826, that the Bank began to wage a war against the discounting houses and the

joint stock banks which ended in "a highly involved tri-
angular action in which the first all but eliminated the second,
and so made the third subject to itself." [22]

FIRST CONSIDERATIONS OF AN ACTIVE FUNCTION OF INTEREST
In connection with the granting of "excessive" commercial
loans by the Bank of England, attacks upon the prevailing
notions of the function of interest were made. The current
doctrine had been that

the whole paper money of every kind which can easily circulate in
any country never can exceed the value of gold and silver, of
which it supplies the place. Should the circulating paper at any
time exceed that sum . . . it must immediately return upon the
banks to be exchanged for gold and silver.[23]

Obviously, the implication of this law was that abundance of
money existed at the time of its operations only as far as the
demand for money was concerned, but that this demand was
not meeting an equally abundant supply. The operation of
the Usury Laws in England at that period prevented, at least
to a certain extent, this condition from resulting in a serious
throttling of a healthy expansion in production or at least in
an undue increase in the price for the capital necessary for
this expansion.[24] No wonder, then, that Adam Smith did not

[22] Newbold, *Democracy, Debts, and Disarmament*, p. 17.

[23] Smith, *The Wealth of Nations*, Book II, chap. ii, p. 283.

[24] Sir Josiah Child, in his tract "A New Discourse of Trade," published in
1688 under the title "Some Brief Observations concerning Trade and Interest
of Money," pp. 7–16, writes that he believes "that the low rate of interest had
largely contributed to the prosperity of Holland, and considering the 6 percent limit too high proposed an additional reduction to 4 percent., which he
calculated would double the national wealth in twenty years" (Andreades,
History of the Bank of England, 1640–1903, tr. by Christabel Meredith),
indicating that one hundred years before Adam Smith the problem in connection with money (*i.e.*, bullion) had been that it (money) existed in too small
amounts. As to how small the danger of excess was considered, compare
Sir William Petty, *Quantuluncunque*, p. 26; *see also* Locke, (*Works*, p. 6)
"Some Considerations of the Lowering of Interest and Raising the Value of
Money." These argued that the rate of interest should be lowered in order
to relieve the prevailing scarcity of money and to have it stream from the
lenders to the tradesmen and the country rather than to the bankers and
London. But it would be mistaken to infer from this that Locke was arguing
a theory of interest. He was arguing against a medieval restriction. As far as
the function of interest was concerned, he recognized quite clearly "the fall

find it necessary to develop a special theory of interest at a time in which interest actually did not as yet play any decisive, functional role. At the turn of the century the intensity of the demand for money had not slackened, but the facilities for supplying the demand had developed greatly. Thus, the venerable directors of the Bank of England combined with the merchants when the latter began to observe with pain the discrepancy between the interest allowed under the Usury Laws and the amount of profit which they had been able to gain from trade for a considerable time. This was especially true in time of war when overseas trade profits were reduced by increasing risks. Thus, very gradually, but nonetheless determinedly, there began an advocacy of the repeal of the Usury Laws.

Mr. Thornton was one of the first to offer theoretical arguments in defense of this position. He maintained that

in order to ascertain how far the desire of obtaining loans at the Bank may be expected at any time to be carried, we must inquire into the subject of the quantum of profit likely to be derived from the borrowing of the existing circumstances. . . . We may . . . consider this question as turning principally upon a comparison of the rate of interest taken at the Bank with the current rate of mercantile profit.[25]

Viner dismisses rather easily the answer which the Bank of England officials gave to these and similar statements before the Bullion Committee when they were denying

that the security against over-issue by the Bank would be reduced if the discount rate were to be lowered from five to four or even to three percent. No person, they insisted, would pay interest for a loan he did not need, whatever the rate, unless it were for the purpose of employing it in speculation, "and provided the conduct of the Bank is regulated as it now is, no accommodation would be given to a person of that description." [26]

. . . or rise of interest, making immediately by its change neither more nor less land, money, or any sort of commodity in England, than there was before, alters not at all the value of money, in reference to commodities" (p. 16).

[25] Thornton, *An Enquiry into . . . Paper Credit*, p. 287.

[26] Cf. Viner, *Studies in the Theory of International Trade*, p. 151; also *Report of the Bullion Committee, 1810, Minutes of Evidence*, p. 129.

It is hard to see how, under the conditions of a healthy industrial expansion and adequately available money, the interest rate could possibly play any important regulatory role if the officials of the Bank spoke with sincerity. No regulative check for the expansion of credit is necessary other than the investigation into the productive and nonspeculative character of the loan. If the rate of interest were higher, it could result only in an increase in the cost of production of the commodities, which latter would amount to a factual decrease in the rate of interest, or it might result in a decrease in the rate of industrial expansion. Ricardo seems to be clearer on this point when he writes: "If the mines had been ten times more productive, ten times more money would the same commerce employ," [27] and publicly, he said once that "what the directors thought a check, namely, the rate of interest on money, was no check at all to the amount of issues, as Adam Smith, Mr. Hume and others had satisfactorily proved." [28] It does not seem that a reference to Ricardo's *Principles* is directly relevant here; namely, that

The applications to the Bank for money . . . depend on the comparison between the rate of profit . . . and the rate at which they are willing to lend it. If they charge less than the market rate of interest, there is no amount of money which they might not lend,—if they charge more than that rate, none but spendthrifts and prodigals would be found to borrow from them.[29]

It is true that Ricardo suggested that a discount rate below the rate of interest would enable otherwise submarginal establishments to continue production. However, as far as "the whole business which the whole community can carry on" is concerned, it

depends on the quantity of its capital; that is, of its raw material, machinery, food, vessels, etc., employed in production. After a well-regulated paper money is established, these can neither be increased nor diminished by the operations of banking. If, then,

[27] Ricardo, *Works*, p. 341.
[28] Hansard, *Parliamentary Debates*, First Series, XL, 744.
[29] Ricardo, "Principles of Political Economy and Taxation," in his *Works*, p. 220.

the state were to issue the paper money of the country, although it should never discount a bill, or lend one shilling to the public, there would be no alteration in the amount of trade . . . and it is probable, too, that the same amount of money might be lent.[30]

To be sure, a large number of modern economists still accept the theory that the quantity of bank loans demanded is dependent on the rate of discount.[31] The validity of that theory will not be contested at present. But it is of interest to follow the development of this notion, so widely accepted today, and to see those conditions gradually emerge—and subside—under which theories of interest could only have been formulated. Stating it this way means emphasizing the fact that there were new conditions under which such a function of the rate of interest as asserted did not exist and, furthermore, that these developed in the first decades of the eighteenth century.

THE CHARACTER OF THE RISE OF THE GENERAL PRICE LEVEL
The only way to shed some light upon the problem of responsibility for changes in prices is to investigate the concrete activities of the country banks, in an attempt to circumscribe their sphere of influence and to determine the degree of interaction between the country banks and the Bank of England. Primarily it was the developing industry which insisted upon the creation of adequate monetary facilities. As Grindon put it, "Financially the cotton trade floated into the atmosphere of life upon wings—wings of paper—money, for coin . . . was a scarce commodity." [32] And he might have added that the existing transportation facilities did not allow for any real import services from the banking institutions existing in the metropolis. Production and banking were often identified; they began to separate slowly in the period with which we are concerned.

It seems only natural that in a period of quick and large-scale expansion many business ventures bordered closely upon

30 Ricardo, *Works*, p. 221.
31 Viner, *Studies in the Theory of International Trade*, p. 151.
32 *Cf.*, Grindon, *Manchester Banks and Bankers*, p. 40.

what today would be called speculation. For example, the banking house of Messrs. Daintry and Ryle of Macclesfield, with its bank at Manchester, incurred heavy losses because of an advance which they had made for a scheme to run steam carriages on ordinary turnpikes "which, when first proposed, seemed to promise certain success." [33]

Such an enterprise seems, from the point of view of our times, to have been rather insecure. If we can accept the fact that any process of expansion will show such unevenness, the problem of that time, especially as far as country banking is concerned, will appear in a different light. To that time the normal trend was expansion, not equilibrium, and expansion was accompanied by the phenomena which we have indicated.

This is of acute interest in allocating the responsibility for the increase in prices in England as they occurred during the period under observation, that is, the restriction period. The antibullionists had claimed that where paper money was issued by the banks solely upon the discount of sound and genuine commercial paper, no excess issue could take place. On this line of reasoning [34] they came to the conclusion that the increase in prices could not have been the result of over-issue.

The implication is that only "sound" commercial paper was being discounted. But what constituted sound paper at that time? As we have indicated above, many of the business ventures appeared to be perfectly sound in that period of quick but intermittent expansion, although they did not necessarily turn out to be sound at all. This necessary limitation upon the argument of the antibullionists must be carried one step farther by distinguishing clearly the two spheres to which the argument concerning the relation between the changing volume of money and price reactions is related. As far as a considerable part of the commodities whose prices were rele-

[33] *Ibid.*, p. 115.
[34] Trawter, *The Principle of Currency and Exchange;* Hill, *An Inquiry into the Causes of the Present High Price of Gold Bullion;* also Bosanquet, *Practical Observations on the Report of the Bullion Committee.*

vant were concerned, they were consumed at or very near the places of their production. Furthermore, the relatively undeveloped system of transportation and communication necessarily made for a much larger independence of each part of the country, with the result that tendencies toward the establishment of a general price level were faint and observable only after a considerable length of time.

Lastly, we may point out in this connection that the inference that relations between *different countries* are comparable to relations between different areas *within one country* had not yet been proved. If we point out the difficulties that such a generalization encounters, we should remember that the dynamic forces working within these two different fields were of a different character. In the relation between two countries, that is, between England and any other country, the objective was at that time exchange, and the side interest of those who were engaged in this activity was the financing of international trade. Capital export was not yet taking place to any appreciable extent. Only after the latter had become an inherent part of international industrial production was the basis for analogy insured.[35]

It is interesting in this connection to see what Silberling says about Ricardo and those who held membership in the Stock Exchange in London. There were two main factions among the members:

Contractors to public loans, who naturally took the bull side of the market, and the professional broker-jobbers who took the bear side in order to derive profits on "continuations." This group borrowed money at five per cent (the maximum legal rate) from local and provincial bankers, and loaned it—*with no limit to the possible rate* [italics by Silberling] to the public, who purchased government stock (the principal type of security traded in at this time) upon an installment or margin basis.[36]

[35] Cf. Niebyl, "Historijske Izmjene u Funkciji Izvoza Kapitala," *Ekonomist* (Zagreb), V, Nos. 7–8 (July–August, 1939), 284–292.

[36] Silberling, "Financial and Monetary Policy," p. 427; see also the evidence given by Ricardo and others to the Commons Committee on the Usury Laws in 1818.

This economic function of the bullionists, by the way, also throws some light upon their position on the question of interest.[37]

The bullionists' position on the possible explanation of the increase in the price level underwent a change while the controversy was still in progress. Boyd clearly stated that the country banks were unable to grant credits in excess of their local demands, since they had not been legally restricted to making cash payments and their customers were free to demand payments in cash. Even if credit for speculative purposes were created, the overissue to each locality would automatically be contracted by demands for cash or Bank of England notes, for instance, by London: "no part of their issue can possibly remain in circulation beyond what the increase in prosperity and industry of the country where they circulate can fairly absorb or digest." [38] By inference this takes cognizance quite correctly of the fact that a healthy expansion of industry cannot possibly create inflation when the expansion is being financed by a necessarily increased amount of credit—in this case paper-money circulation.

Thornton was, perhaps, the first one to fall prey to the temptation to identify money circulation in the provinces and the functioning of money in international exchange, which is functionally inadmissible. There is no doubt that the financial structure of England was gradually developing toward centralization, but to state that the Bank of England was already the basis and the controlling influence of the country's entire credit circulation was far overstating the case as it was at that time.[39] Thornton's vision is admirable in seeing the

[37] See previous reference to the bullionists' position on interest, p. 68.

[38] Quoted by Silberling, in "Financial and Monetary Policy of Great Britain," p. 405.

[39] See Boyd's *Letter to . . . Pitt,* p. 20. "The Bank of England is a great source of all the circulation of the country; and, by the increase or diminution of its paper, the increase or diminution of every country bank is infallibly regulated." As Silberling has pointed out, it was not Boyd's intention to exonerate the country banks because he preferred them. It was rather because of his hate of the Bank of England, which he held responsible for his own financial collapse, that he tried to fix the responsibility upon the latter. As

outline of the things in process and to come, but he exhibits here a fundamental shortcoming in entirely neglecting what actually was happening within the process of production. He preferred intellectual speculation about the possible relations between the multitude of monetary surface phenomena.

As far as the development of the monetary relations in international trade is concerned, the bullionists, especially Thornton, contributed extensively to our knowledge of these processes. Thornton postulated the principle of a monetary equilibrium in commercially, but not yet productively, interconnected areas. Here he explained conclusively, on the basis of what may be called a purchasing-power parity theory, that in nations having a metallic standard precious metals would always tend to be evenly distributed, since great disparity would tend to increase or to decrease commodity prices. We should remember, again, that the prices to which Thornton refers are only those of commodities in international trade and that these are not necessarily relevant to the provinces.[40] Ricardo reasoned in much the same way.[41]

The conclusion we come to can be summarized as follows. There was no doubt but that prices in England tended to increase. This tendency was occasioned by two different and not directly connected causes. The increase of the prices in international trade was largely due to the extraordinary credits which the government had been forced to take out in order to finance the war and the equally extraordinary remittances to foreign countries in order to pay either directly for the expenses of the English armies or indirectly to subsidize those nations which were on the side of the English commercial interests. The increase, and even more the fluctuations of the prices in the provinces of England, have to be explained

we point out, this statement of Boyd's, whatever its psychological foundation, coincides with our contention that as far as the problem of excess issue manifested in the international exchange rates was concerned, this had to be traced primarily, if not exclusively, to the operations of the Bank of England, not to the credit operations of the country banks.

[40] Thornton, *Paper Credit*, pp. 115 ff.
[41] Ricardo, "High Price of Bullion," in his *Works*, pp. 275 ff.

primarily with reference to the productive expansion, whose very character was at that time to proceed spasmodically, because of the necessarily anticipatory character of investment, which bordered on and was in many cases identical with speculation.[42]

INFLATION AND ITS EFFECTS: THE THEORY OF FORCED SAVINGS

The effect of the increase in prices upon industry did not go unnoticed, as Professor Hayek[43] has rediscovered. Hayek quotes extensively Jeremy Bentham, who in his *Manual of Political Economy*[44] traces the effects of increasing prices through the creation of paper money and the distribution of these effects as "forced frugality."

The effect of every increase of money (understand, of the ratio of the quantity of things vendible, to the quantity of things vendible for money) is to impose an unprofitable income tax on the incomes of all fixed incomists.[45]

Malthus pointed out that:

The new notes go into the market, as so much additional capital, to purchase what is necessary for the conduct of the concern. But before the produce of the country has been increased, it is impossible for one person to have more of it, without diminishing the shares of some others. This diminution is effected by the rise of prices, occasioned by the competition of the new notes, which put it out of the power of those who are only buyers, and not sellers, to purchase as much of the annual produce as before.[46]

Both agree, in the words of Bentham, that "in the above case of forced frugality, national wealth is increased," or in Malthus's terms, that "all those who sell as well as buy, are, during the progressive rise of prices making unusual profits; and, even when this progression stops, are left with a com-

---

[42] Cf. Silberling, "Financial and Monetary Policy of Great Britain," p. 420n. "It was found that the quarterly cyclical fluctuations in the country notes *preceded,* or *synchronized with,* those of wholesale commodity prices."

[43] Von Hayek, "A Note on the Development of the Doctrine of 'Forced Saving,'" in *Quarterly Journal of Economics,* XLVII (1932), 123–133.

[44] Bentham, *The Works of Jeremy Bentham,* ed. John Bowring, III, 31–84.

[45] Viner, *Studies in the Theory of International Trade,* p. 188, quotes Jeremy Bentham, *The Rationale of Reward,* pp. 312–313.

[46] *The Edinburgh Review,* XVII (February, 1811), 364 ff.

mand of a greater portion of the annual produce than they possessed previous to the new issues." [47]

Henry Thornton, Dugald Stewart, and Lauderdale argue in much the same way. We find in each, however, a considerable critique of such procedure. Henry Thornton had pointed out that "this saving, as well as any additional one which may arise from a similar defalcation of the revenue of the unproductive members of the society, will be attended with a proportionate hardship and injustice." [48] And Lauderdale says that:

The radical evil . . . seems to be, not the mere overissue of notes, considered as an addition to our currency, but the anomalous and unchecked extension of *credit* and its inevitable effect of producing a sudden augmentation in prices by a sudden augmentation of demand.[49]

These positions were taken on the basis of a clearer realization of the nature of the inflationary character of the note circulation at that time. We say consciously "clearer" understanding, because as we have pointed out previously and as Stewart himself has pointed out in discussing Thornton's opinions in the Bullion Report, Thornton was not fully aware of the relations between the process of production and the volume of the means of exchange extant. To put it in Stewart's own words:

If . . . this excess be only symptomatic of another malady, with which, from particular circumstances, it happens to be co-existent (of an extension of credit, to wit, calculated to derange the pre-existing relations of demand and supply) then in that case the restriction and *regulation* of this credit, ought to be regarded as the primary object, and the reduction of our circulating medium attended to solely as an indication that the cure is progressive.[50]

Stewart focuses his attention upon credit, whereas he really should have been concerned with the causes which gave rise

[47] *Ibid.*   [48] Thornton, *An Enquiry into . . . Paper Credit*, p. 263.
[49] Stewart, *The Collected Works*, ed. by Sir William Hamilton, p. 440; attention has been drawn to these citations by Professor Hayek in his "Note on . . . Forced Savings."
[50] *Ibid.*, p. 443.

to this credit expansion; here we are back to the argument which we have put forward earlier—that the type of industrial development needed just this kind of credit expansion.

Professor Viner has drawn attention to the fact that there exists another version of the theory of inflation, and he quotes Thompson and Burgess.[51] According to them, the increased volume of money would result in increased employment in the production of consumers' goods, and thus the prices would rise rather slowly because of the increased supply. There seems to be no reason for these views to conflict. Neither do they coincide nor contradict, but rather complement each other.

SOME TENTATIVE CONCLUSIONS ON THE CLASSICAL THEORY OF INFLATION   1) In our analysis of the classical theory of inflation we demonstrated first that the "received doctrine" concerning money in the period under consideration had been formulated under mercantile conditions based on a manufactural, not an industrial, mode of production. The newly developing general economic theory concentrated on the problem of production in accordance with the relative scarcity of labor, which was the concrete major problem of its time. It was in this situation that the intermittent industrial expansion, enhanced by the specific conditions of the Anglo-French wars, resulted in a general rise of prices.

The analysis of this phenomenon of rising prices was carried on by a scientific method which could not yet include the concept of qualitative change. On the contrary, "received doctrine," as well as the outward appearance of the economic process, seemed to suggest merely quantitative expansion without any apparent fundamental qualitative change in the structure of production. The result of such an attitude toward the phenomenon of rising prices was to conceive of them as deviations from an otherwise static condition of

---

[51] Thompson, "On the Instrument of Exchange," *Westminster Review*, I (1824), 200; Henry Burgess, *A Letter to the Right Honorable George Canning*, pp. 79–82. See also Viner, *Studies in the Theory of International Trade*, p. 189.

equilibrium. Such a theoretical position was not obviously fallacious for that time because the actual, though temporary, economic conditions tended to obscure the imminent structural change indicated by the rise of prices.

2) From the foregoing presentation of the main elements of the classical theory of inflation, some conclusions pertinent to theory formation today can be drawn. We found that each one of the main concepts developed and subsequently employed was relative to and inseparable from a particular set of circumstances. These circumstances were not "particular" in the sense of "accidental," but form a consistent, while at the same time qualitatively changing, pattern. Having been created for the solution of concrete problems immanent in this pattern and reflecting this pattern in turn in their logic, the conclusion is forced upon us that these economic concepts, and by inference the concepts of other disciplines, must change correlatively.[52]

More particularly, we found that the significance of inflation-like phenomena depends upon the character of the concrete stage of the qualitatively changing process of production. In early industrial production the possible and actually occurring expansion justified the assumptions of (a) a quasi-equilibrium and (b) a relatively high and still increasing degree of unfettered interdependence of the factors of production. A monetary theory, therefore, based on these assumptions necessarily had to coincide with a high degree of accuracy with the concrete economic events at that time.

The classical theory of inflation expressed thus merely the phenomenal coincidence of a specific historical period. It should be understood as a "special case" in doctrine formation created by and applicable to a special historical situation only. This, however, inferentially amounts to saying that the absence of the same conditions necessitates the formulation of correspondingly different concepts.[53]

[52] Niebyl, "The Need for a Concept of Value in Economic Theory," *Quarterly Journal of Economics*, LIV, Part 2 (February, 1940), 201–216.

[53] For a recent statement of a different point of view see Marget, *The Theory of Prices*, Vol. I.

7 · The Economic Setting of Deflation

THE report of the Bullion Committee was made to Parliament in 1810. Attention is usually called to the depression of 1810 and how it delayed governmental action on the revocation of the Restriction Bill. Napoleon's reappearance in 1815 is considered a cause for the further postponement of the resumption of cash payments. Only in 1819 the law was passed by Parliament whereby the Bank of England had to redeem its notes in gold, to be specific, in gold ingots. Parallel with this overhesitant performance of the government runs a somewhat more determined policy of the directors of the Bank of England. This institution began in 1817 to redeem Bank of England notes below £5. As an apparent aftermath of these events, there appeared a discount of the English exchange as against foreign exchanges, with the explanation for which English bankers and business men were soon seriously concerned.

What then are the relevant factors to be taken into account if we are to understand the economic effects of the monetary policies of the time? Monetary historians and theorists began to emphasize monetary data to the exclusion of other data when attempting to bring light into the mysteries of the flow of money. It seems to us that at this point it is necessary to discuss the again changing general economic situation of England before we can concern ourselves with the *particular* causes affecting the flow of money and the results of the conscious direction given to this flow by government as well as by business. In the process of this analysis we shall be able to discern and to understand the nature of the monetary theories advanced during this period.

THE CHANGING PROCESS OF PRODUCTION   The Industrial Revolution is usually said to have begun on the date of Watt's invention of his improved steam engine. A fact that is often disregarded in such presentations is that inventions do not appear without due preparation inherent in the historical changes of the economic and social structure. For example, the application of power machines, such as Watt's improved steam engine, was possible only after a large number of tool machines had been created which were capable of being co-ordinated by means of a central power machine. When this was accomplished, the next problem was to reproduce these machines on a large scale. Machines had to be produced by machines, and it was not until the beginning of the nineteenth century that the technique was developed whereby machine tools were produced by means of other machines. The important datum for us at the moment is that this process did not become general before the beginning of the nineteenth century.

But let us look at another aspect of this early stage of this period; let us take the worker and his changing function within this process. As long as the laborer worked with individual tools, the "capital" invested in these tools was relatively small. With the advent of machinery, the volume of capital invested in production necessarily increased with the number of increasingly complex machines used in production. Not only the necessary volume of capital increased but also its fixity. It is true that some machine tools were used for a single process of producing one certain commodity, but it is more important that they were now used ever increasingly for series of processes.

As Mr. Ashworth, an important cotton manufacturer of that period, said: "When a laborer lays down his spade he renders useless, for that period, a capital worth 18d. When one of our people leaves the mill he renders useless a capital that has cost 100,000 pounds.[1] The result, as far as it affected the laborer, was to make it desirable for the employer to prolong the work day in order to make profits on the investment of an ever-larger volume of fixed capital. The process found its natural limitation in the physical capacity of the worker. As a result the shortening of excessively long periods of labor demanded by the laborers became less stubbornly opposed by

[1] Senior, *Letters on the Factory Act,* pp. 13–14.

the employers. The latter began to realize that an optimum of output was not reachable by a mere quantitative extension of the laboring day.[2]

Accompanying this process of the mechanization of industry was the emigration of the laborer from the countryside to the towns, which reached the end of its first stage at this time. Concentration of labor in the towns created a market which for the time being definitely re-established the prosperity of English agriculture. It was more important, however, that it now was possible for industry to reproduce its own industrial reserve army by setting labor free in the competitive process of improving its technological equipment. In this way it began to supply the less urgently demanded labor for the still-continuing increase in the volume of production.[3]

[2] It is obvious that the process of learning the skill needed in industry was quite a lengthy one. Boulton and Watt, for instance, were ever ready to complain about the lack of skill of their new workmen. See also the system of divided labor introduced by Wedgwood in his factory (Meteyard, *The Life of Josiah Wedgwood*, I., 225). In this respect the transformation of England into an industrialized country differs in no way from the phenomenon observable in the USSR in the recent past. In England the intensity of this lack of skilled labor, including draughtsmen and clerks, began to subside with the turn of the eighteenth century (Lord, *Capital and Steam-Power*, p. 200).

[3] Technological displacement and population growth at that time represent problems to which Malthus, among others, attempted to give an answer in his crude population theory. He conceived quite correctly the direct dependence of the rate of population growth or decline upon the existing economic conditions. His particular way of exposing this dependence, that is, his juxtaposition of quantitative arithmetic and geometric series exhibited in the relation of agricultural output and number of population is, however, quite irrelevant to his main point, namely, that this dependence *exists*. Only a later age, which looked upon quantitative investigation as a shibboleth for "science," could be misled far enough to become gravely concerned over such a purely phenomenal problem.

Malthus's theory of population, as compared to that of Petty, for instance, shows clearly the complete qualitative change which population theory, along with economic reality, had undergone. As an apologist for the *status quo ante*, that is, scarcity of labor supply, wages at a point necessary for reproduction of physical energy, and no government assistance to the unemployed, Malthus tried to deal with population growth and the ensuing misery of the people as pessimistically as Petty had been optimistic in his advocacy of an increasing population.

Ricardo saw this process much more clearly than the polemicizing Malthus. And while Petty gave clear economic reasons for the observed and demanded population growth, Malthus, in his function as an apologist, is forced to resort to an appeal to purely metaphysical "biological" forces.

Ricardo stated clearly: "I have said that when a manufacturer is in pos-

This process of increasing machine production produced unemployment and starvation among the handicraft trades; the death struggle of the weavers of cotton by hand looms is a horrifying example.[4] There we find the foundation for the lagging real wage of the laborers, which in turn made possible, in part, the freeing of production resources demanded for the increasing *investment* needs. The process of economic structural transformation which took place between 1780 and 1810 can best be illustrated by examples. There are as yet, unfortunately, only a few really adequate investigations into the development of business enterprise at that time. The enterprise of Boulton and Watt affords perhaps as typical an illustration of the newly emerging type of production as can be found.[5]

---

session of a circulating capital, he can employ with it a great number of men; and if it should suit his purposes to substitute a fixed capital of an equal value for this circulating capital, it will be inevitably followed by a necessity for dismissing a part of his workmen, for a fixed capital cannot employ all the labour which it is calculated to supersede" (Ricardo to John Ramsay McCulloch, London, 18 June, 1821, in: *Letters of David Ricardo to John Ramsay McCulloch,* 1816–1823, ed. by J. H. Hollander, p. 109). If "these truths appear (to Ricardo) . . . to be as demonstrable as any of the truths of geometry" (*ibid.*) they most certainly are demonstrated today. The kernel of Ricardo's wisdom lies in the fact that he deduced the necessity of a surplus population (in the long run) from the analysis of the mechanics of the system of production.

W. Stanley Jevons, who agreed with Malthus's basic thesis (Jevons, *The Coal Question,* p. 149) remade the pessimism of the latter into a now equally unwarranted optimism. Living in the second youth of industrial society, that is, after the exploitation of the colonies had begun, he regarded "the increase in population . . . rather under than above the increasing means of subsistence (*ibid.*, p. 173). As one of the first advocates of the pleasure-pain principle, that is, of a psychological and purely phenomenal approach in economic analysis, he was unable to see the productive dynamics of the process.

[4] "The price paid for weaving a particular kind of cloth, as shown in the following table, will exhibit the extraordinary depreciation which has taken place in the value of this species of labour:

1795	39/9	(shilling)
1810	15/-	"
1830	5/-	"

"This is not a solitary instance; it is an example of the entire labour connected with hand-loom manufacture." Phillip Gaskell, *Artisans and Machinery.*

[5] Lord, *Capital and Steam Power, 1750–1800,* p. 2; see also the very informative investigation by Erich Roll, *An Early Experiment in Industrial Organization, Being a History of the Firm of Boulton & Watt, 1775–1805.*

James Watt was originally a mathematical instrument maker, whose mind was "directed to the study of the steam-engine" [6] when he had to repair a model of Newcomen's engine belonging to the University of Glasgow. In conjunction with Professor Black of the same university, Watt set out to improve Newcomen's engine. To pursue this work, he was forced to look for financial assistance. It is interesting to see that he found the necessary "capital" in the private fortune of Dr. Black. Later on, after this source had been exhausted, Dr. Roebuck, of the Carron Iron Works,[7] became interested. He had found the steam engine of Newcomen inadequate for pumping his mines clear of water. With the financial collapse of Roebuck,[8] Watt again had to look for a new patron and found him in Mr. Boulton, who owned a very modern hardware factory [9] in Soho, near Birmingham.[10] "All classes of workmen (were) engaged in the manufacture of its various products; and in the owner of this factory was vested the technical as well as the entire economic control over his employees . . . Soho had all the characteristics of a factory, and it carried machine production to a high degree notwithstanding the unreliable power which it could command." [11] It is in this factory that Watt continued his important experiments. The form of partnership into which he entered with Boulton is quite significant for our problem. It was not a partnership designed to produce improved steam engines, but to establish a firm of consulting engineers. The production of steam engines would have required a relatively large amount of capital which was not available, either to the producers or to those who were interested in buying the engines. Whatever capital

[6] Muirhead, *Life of James Watt*, p. 75; see this work also for the interesting capitalization of Watt's business as a mathematical instrument maker.

[7] Erich Roll, *ibid.*, p. 12. For a more detailed account of this enterprise see Lord, *Capital and Steam-Power*, pp. 76 ff. Roebuck, as well as Boulton, had been among the first to localize their industries consciously according to transportation and power facilities rather than by what at least appeared to have been accident.

[8] The financial difficulties of Roebuck's firm are an interesting example of the development of credit in Scotland, which Adam Smith discussed at length (*Wealth of Nations*, I, 281 ff.).

[9] John Lord quotes a letter from M. Boulton to Wendler, July 10, 1767 (Tew. MS), in which Boulton writes about his type of work, "I should be glad to work for all Europe in things they may have occasion for in Gold, Silver, Copper, Plated, Gilt, Pinchbeck, Steel, Platina, Tortoises-shell." Lord, *Capital and Steam-Power*, p. 44.

[10] Birmingham, as a non-chartered town, had been relatively uninhibited in its development as one of the centers for metal work since the sixteenth century. See *The Present State of Birmingham;* Lord, *Capital and Steam-Power*, pp. 39 ff.

[11] Lord, *Capital and Steam-Power*, pp. 5–6.

Boulton was able to raise, privately, by selling parts of his own and his wife's estates, by loans from wealthy private or business friends, from banks, or from recourse to the liquid means of his own factory, was hardly enough to keep the necessary experiments going.

This *lack of capital* was expressed in the *production technique* adopted by Boulton & Watt. They did not produce all the parts in their own factory, as the latter was not properly equipped, and the outlay for a new and complete engine factory would have been far too great. Thus, it was largely left to the discretion of the buyers to secure the parts needed for the engine and specified by Boulton & Watt, with the exception of especially important parts, which they either produced themselves or specified to be ordered from certain establishments. For example, cylinders were ordered from J. Wilkinson, who with his father had been a pioneer in the process of melting metals.[12]

Boulton & Watt succeeded in this way in reducing their own capital investment to a minimum, but they proved their real business genius by recognizing the same necessity for their purchasers. The price they made was based upon the actual cost of the parts which they themselves delivered, plus "$\frac{1}{3}$ of the savings as compared with the consumption of one of Smeaton's engines." [13] This premium was to be paid half-yearly for the duration of the patent which had been granted to Boulton & Watt, by Act of Parliament, for 25 years.[14] This arrangement made it possible for the purchasers to avail themselves of the new engine with no more capital outlay than they would have had to incur in buying the old unimproved type. The additional price for the new engine they were allowed to pay out of the savings which they were able to effect by its employment.

This business technique is typical of a period in which capital was scarce all around. Significantly, we find that this technique changed as soon as the fundamental economic conditions changed.

The period between 1776, the beginning of their partnership,

[12] For his interesting career see Dickinson, *John Wilkinson, Iron Master;* also Paliner, *John Wilkinson and the Old Bersham Iron Works.*

[13] Watt to Wright, 16 April, 1778. Cited by Roll, *An Early Experiment in Industrial Organization,* pp. 109–110: "The real cause of the curious system of payment was, undoubtedly, lack of capital."

[14] The special Act of Extension through which Boulton and Watt received their patent in 1775 is a significant example of a changing function of an economic institution. The privilege of granting monopolies to enterprises had been used since the reign of Elizabeth to improve mercantile activities in England. Now, this monopoly privilege was invoked by pioneering industrial entrepreneurs, to safeguard the infant steps of the age of *laissez faire.*

and the late 1780's, when the business technique was altered, consisted for the firm of Boulton & Watt of a series of financial stringencies, only gradually lessened toward the end of the period. During all this time, the machines were improved and their field of application increased rapidly.[15]

The immediate occasion for the change from a royalty system to a lump-sum premium, that is, to the sale of the machines at a fixed price, was the impending expiration of the patent in 1800. The point not to be lost sight of is that this change in business technique manifested a change in the general economic conditions in as much as it was now possible to (a) produce the machines themselves, because the necessary techniques had been developed, and (b) sell them at a fixed rate, because of the gradually accumulating business profits, that is, an increasing volume of available investment funds. The stage has been reached where we can consider the firm of Boulton & Watt as a productive enterprise, which from this point on was typical of the industrial type of production.[16] There was little difficulty now in securing adequate capital. By 1812, the entire debt to the parent firm, that of Mr. Boulton, Sr., had been paid back.

This case is not to be taken in any absolute sense as representative of the whole development of that time. We are interested in the structural tendencies which undoubtedly found manifold expression in the different types of industry, according to different particular historical situations. What comes out rather clearly is that the infant stage of industrial society was during this period gradually outgrown, and the nature of the demand for capital underwent a considerable change. There can be no doubt that this change in the financial aspects of the productive apparatus of the time had considerable importance with regard to the character of the flow of money and to the reactions which any manipulation of this flow evoked. When Boulton & Watt started business, the capital available was small and was supplied largely by private resources and by the purchasers of their engines, the latter

[15] For example, the epoch-making application of steam power to flour milling, *ibid.*, p. 112.

[16] This typical character was also apparent in the changed character of the owners and operators of the enterprise, Messrs. Boulton, Jr., & Watt, Jr., who were solid business men and no longer inventors like Mr. Watt, Sr., or promoters like Mr. Boulton, Sr.

constituting in effect a peculiar kind of credit. As far as bank loans were concerned, they were granted only after the firm was well under way and then first by London and later by Amsterdam bankers.[17] The necessity for these loans ceased to exist in the last years of the eighteenth century after the country banks had become well established.

For a similar development we may briefly refer to the growth of the famous pottery firm of Josiah Wedgwood. Wedgwood also started with his own small private fortune, supported by friends rather than by bankers. It should be remembered, though, that some of these friends were merchants, such as Bentley, who helped Wedgwood to establish his Etruria works. Bentley was originally a Manchester warehouseman; later he became a general merchant and financier first in Liverpool and later in London. In contrast to Boulton, who had developed into a typical industrial promoter, Wedgwood represented rather "the intermediate state of paternal employer between the guild-master and the pure capitalist." [18]

Wedgwood introduced the first steam engine in his works in 1782, and J. Wilkinson in 1776. The total number of steam engines of the old type working in 1775 was 130. In 1800 there were 321, with a horsepower of 5,210,[19] no longer predominantly in mines, as had been the case earlier, but now employed in textile manufacture, bleaching, the printing of calico, dyeing, and so forth, thus making large-scale production possible.

The growing industries necessitated improvement in transportation. The Bridgewater Canal was constructed mainly by means of funds from the adjoining coal mines, and the Grand Trunk Canal was initiated by Wedgwood.[20] But by 1800 industry had developed generally far enough so that the possibilities of large profits out of investments in transportation

[17] £14,000 from Lowe, Vere & Co., London (Roll, *An Early Experiment in Industrial Organization*, pp. 100 ff.), £7,000 from Wiss, a Dutch banker (see Lord, *Capital and Steam-Power*, pp. 116–117, 120–123), £30,000 or £40,000 from Mr. Hope, an Amsterdam banker (*ibid.*, p. 133).

[18] Lord, *Capital and Steam-Power*, pp. 143, 185.   [19] *Ibid.*, p. 176.

[20] *The Present State of Birmingham*, p. 21.

began to attract speculation, with the usual result that the anticipations outran the actual immediate needs. Here, again, we have an example of what so often is lightly dismissed as "irresponsible," "uneconomic," and "avoidable" speculation but which in reality represents an indispensable step in the growth of industrial capitalism.

The point of our brief historical illustration may be summarized in this way. With the turn of the century, industry in England had reached a stage in its development that was functionally and basically different from that of twenty-five years earlier. "By the year 1800, the steam-engine had not made such a transformation in industry as is often imagined, nor, on the other hand, was it so defective as to be relatively unimportant." [21] The stage was set, however, for a development that was to be as different from the preceding one as the theory and the understanding of the function of money in David Hume's and Adam Smith's time were to differ from that of the deflation period and currency debates after the resumption of cash payments by the Bank of England.

THE FUNCTION OF BILL-BROKING   The two outstanding types of institution relevant to the change in the function of money were the bill-broking houses and the joint-stock industrial as well as banking establishments.

We have pointed out before [22] that the use of bills for obtaining liquid funds was not as such a development characteristic of the last quarter of the eighteenth century. The technique of using commercial bills had been employed previously between private traders and even between individual merchants and individual producers of the mercantile and manufacturing type. As long as the trade in bills was dependent upon the direct exchange between economic *individuals,* the sphere of their circulation, and therewith their total amount and their importance as a part of the volume of money in circulation, was restricted.

[21] Lord, *Capital and Steam-Power,* p. 221.   [22] *Ibid.,* p. 23.

It was only after the rise of financial institutions adequate for the period, of which the country banks were the first to emerge, that the technique of financing economic transactions by means of bills found a base upon which it could prosper. It has been said that direct bank loans and overdrafts, the latter especially in Scotland, were primarily used for the accommodation of immediate cash needs: for instance, for wage payments, and so forth. The larger amounts were almost exclusively secured by means of drawing bills. It was a function of country banks to transform these bills into cash for their clients, which they accomplished if there were no ready cash on hand by giving their own drafts to their London correspondents.

There is one characteristic of country banking which proved to be of considerable importance in the development of bill-broking houses. This was the interpretation of the Acts of Parliament of 1708 and 1742, by which the monopoly on the issuing of notes of the Bank of England had been protected by means of forbidding all other banks to have more than six partners, thus restricting the possible growth of any rival banks. In the beginning of the development of country banks the common function of all banks had been to issue notes. However, the restriction in size was applied to all banks, including those institutions later developed which were not predominantly interested in the issuing of notes. The result of this interpretation of the Acts was that with the growth of industrial and commercial transactions the country banks found it difficult to adjust their own capital to their expanded business.[23] They were forced to rely increasingly upon their London connections for the remunerative disposal of their

---

[23] This influence of the Acts of 1708 and 1742 upon the forms of the financial institutions which emerged from the changed conditions is a rather clear case of an influence of institutions developed in a preceding period for the purpose of dealing with problems of that preceding period, upon the forms of the institutions in the succeeding period created to deal with the problems of that period. It should be noted clearly that this influence affected, in this case as always, only the forms, not the functional content, of the new institutions.

country funds, as well as for securing such funds when needed.[24]

The funds sent to London by the country bankers were usually allowed some interest by the London bankers with whom they had been deposited. This continued as long as relative scarcity of funds generally prevailed. After the restriction of cash payments in 1797 the Bank of England began to accommodate the financial needs by issuing paper. The result was a plentiful supply of money, which made it difficult for the London banks to employ remuneratively the country funds deposited with them. It should be noted that the practice of issuing bills had been followed by the country banks for some time, and they were enlarging upon it when the Bank of England began its competition. Exchequer bills which had been employed in the investment of bank balances began to fall and with them the interest rates, with the result that the London bankers abandoned the practice of paying interest on the deposits of the country banks. The country banks were thus forced to look for direct investment for their funds, and since their localized status and experience did not permit them a wide enough range for the procurement of investment prospects, they began to employ London agents who made it their special business to perform such tasks.

It would be a mistake to assume that all these country banks were alike. We have referred elsewhere to the development of English foreign trade during this period. The increase in the political and to a certain extent commercial difficulties between England, on the one side, and Holland and France on the other,[25] as well as the invention of the cotton gin by Eli

[24] See the evidence of Bagehot before the "Select Committee of the Restrictions Imposed and Privileges Conferred by Law on Bankers Authorized to Make and Issue Notes in England, Scotland, and Ireland Respectively," *British Parliamentary Papers*, 1775 (351), IX. 1. *Minutes*, 7999.

[25] The disturbances of the commercial relations between England and France during the war must not be overemphasized. Thus, for instance, the British insured the French ships in the West Indies trade in the midst of the Anglo-French wars as a result of which the French did not even care to convoy these vessels (*Essays on the Science of Insurance, Whether It Be Nationally Advantageous to Insure the Ships of Our Foreign Enemies*, 1797, pp. 7–16; also Boulton and Watt delivered an 85 horse-power engine in

Whitney, had increased the trade between Liverpool and Philadelphia. This trade was financed largely by bills of the Quakers on both sides of the Atlantic. Country banks such as that of Gurnell, Hoare, and Harman, with connections in neutral Hamburg—Amsterdam and Rotterdam being blockaded—rose to power.[26]

The same development, to varying extents, could be observed in other trade ports. The rise of Gurnell and Company of Norwich offers a good example.[27] They had been engaged in the wool trade originally and had gone through the stage of supplying domestic producers with the necessary funds; finally they established the Norwich and Norfolk Bank. Their London correspondent was a Joseph Smith, who himself was a wool factor.[28] By 1799 Smith, who had received in his business many bills from other provincial banks which he had furnished to Gurnell for the employment of their funds, began to concentrate on the banking business. For the bills which he furnished to Gurnell he charged a commission of one-fourth of one percent. The business increased, and in 1802 Thomas Richardson, a former clerk of Smith & Holt, began to accommodate Gurnell with bills, charging no commission to Gurnell, the lender of the money, but receiving his income entirely from the borrowers in the form of brokerage. The business flourished so well that in 1807 the Gurnell family itself became represented in the brokerage firm of Richardson. The bill-broking house of Richardson transacted bills at that time to the amount of £1,450,000. King computed the turnover of this firm in 1813 as more than £17,500,000. After 1810 the bill-brokers were in a position to penetrate directly into the main industrial areas, because the character of the country banks and the resultant discount policy had

---

1779 to Paris after having obtained official passports (see Lord, *Capital and Steam-Power*, p. 211). John Lord (*ibid.*, p. 227) mentions also that even "wars are delayed because nations have insured themselves (Aris, *Birmingham Gazette*, March 23, 1778). Arms and goods are sold to opponents."

[26] Newbold, *Democracy, Debts and Disarmament*, p. 16.

[27] Bourne, *English Merchants*, pp. 356 ff.

[28] W. T. C. King, *History of the London Discount Market*, p. 18.

not proved capable of adequately accommodating the needs of the enormously expanding industry. The bank rate was kept at 5 percent, and when the economic difficulties in 1817 created another oversupply of investible funds, the bill-broking houses were quick to take advantage of the situation by reducing their interest rate. The policy of the Bank of England here again played an important role. We mentioned before that the Bank of England had begun to discount bills after the suspension of cash payments in 1797. The competition of the private bill brokers became marked after 1810 causing the portfolio of the Bank of England to fall off considerably, since the Bank adhered strictly to its discount rate of 5 percent.[29] It is interesting to see that "by the middle of 1819, he [Gurnell] was complaining of a shortage, not of bills, but of money, which he attributed to the inadequacy of circulation." [30] We shall come back later to the cause and other effects of this shortage of money.

Another cause of the decrease in importance of the discount business of the Bank of England was the policy of the Bank not to accept any paper running for more than 65 days. The character of the newly developing finance was such that this period proved for the most part to be insufficient, and while the Bank of England adhered strictly to its established policy, the bill brokers were willing to accommodate according to the quality of the paper rather than according to the length of its run. While it may be assumed that the average discounts were about three months, bills were discounted by the brokerage houses for as long a period as three years.

The country banks which had been established and now functioned in developing industrialized areas were confronted, as we have pointed out before, with the need to furnish the circulating capital for the growing industrial

[29] Lord's "Committee on the State of the Bank of England with Reference to the Expediency of the Resumption of Cash Payments," *British Parliamentary Papers,* 1819 (291) III, 363–(47).

[30] W. T. C. King, *History of the London Discount Market,* p. 29; "Secret Committee on the Expediency of the Bank Resuming Cash Payments," *British Parliamentary Papers,* 1819 (202), III, 1–(46), and 1819 (282) III, 1–(46).

enterprises. Consequently, they issued bills of rather small denominations, especially in Lancashire, where notes were issued rather hesitatingly. These bills actually functioned as currency. The use of such very small bills was somewhat discouraged after 1815, because of an increase in the stamp duties for bills under £20.

Many of these bills found their way to the larger import merchants in the ports and from there to London. Their quality could not easily be appraised so far from their place of issue except by specialists, an occupation which was also increasingly taken over by the bill brokers. "Regular customers invariably relied upon the bill-broker's judgment, and would take from him paper which would have been rejected unhesitatingly had it been taken direct." [31] All these functions of the bill brokers tended to improve the discount facilities for the manufacturer in the country,[32] and thus to provide for the emerging needs described above for fixed as well as circulating capital. For the country banks the establishment of the London bill brokers was important, since they offered an expert knowledge of the paper dealt in, which made for a marked decrease in the losses compared to those incurred before their advent, and, secondly, because they served as a ready market for the disposal of bills.

JOINT-STOCK ENTERPRISE AND JOINT-STOCK BANKING The gradual emergence of industrial production had brought the invention of power as the technical basis for production. It had now become possible to extend the process of dividing labor and to concentrate production in larger establishments. We have already discussed some of the financial problems which arose within this process. The duty of securing the necessary capital rested entirely with the owner of the enterprise. While the banks were willing to supply much of the circulating capital, fixed capital in most cases had to be pro-

---

[31] W. T. C. King, *History of the London Discount Market*, p. 33.
[32] See report of "Select Committee on the High Price of Bullion," *British Parliamentary Papers*, 1813 (349), III, 1–48.

vided through direct loans. It was in line with the development of the industrial structure, therefore, that gradually an accepted form developed whereby recapitalization, as well as the securing of new capital, for the constantly expanding and newly developing enterprises took place. This form was a mere institutionalization and legalization of existing practices. The private lenders of money for purposes of industrial production received in return part of the profits made out of the application of their capital to production. They were increasingly hesitant to incur any personal liability for the entire obligations of the enterprise in which their capital was working. The limited liability joint-stock companies exhibit exactly the desired features of limited liability, with the one difference that instead of the general custom of guaranteeing interest returns the "silent" partners in a joint-stock company were made to participate in whatever profits the enterprise was capable of producing. Furthermore, financial stability of the enterprises was enforced by having the capital that was formerly borrowed for a limited period of time now invested as part of the permanent fixed capital.

Lastly, continuity in enterprise was made possible through the joint-stock form. The individual entrepreneur could offer no guarantee for the continuation of his enterprise, and it was for the sake of the continuity of the returns of invested capital in case of accidents happening to such an entrepreneur that the joint-stock form of enterprise represents the definite emancipation of production as an active economic unit independent of the individual personnel of its leadership. The anonymity of enterprise thus created is the necessary complement to absentee owner capital, whose influence in the later development of industrial society was to become of such marked importance.[33]

It is interesting to observe that the clause "limited liability" was introduced first in France, offering an example that "late" industrial countries were more likely to introduce rather

[33] Veblen, *The Theory of Business Enterprise;* also *The Theory of the Leisure Class.*

radical changes in their existing legal patterns than the countries which, like England, gradually developed new economic institutions. While England did not sanction limited liability until 1855, joint-stock companies in industry began to grow long before that time.

The Bubble Act of 1719 had checked the use of the unincorporated joint-stock companies as applied to mercantile business.[34] However, the Act had been drawn up in such an "unintelligible" way [35] that when the economic necessity arose the Act itself was simply circumvented.[36] A large number of companies were incorporated, but an even larger number of joint-stock manufacturing and trading companies did not bother to incorporate. There was only one prosecution under the Bubble Act up to 1808. By 1825 joint-stock companies representing capital of about £200,000,000 were said to have existed,[37] and when at that time attempts were made to enforce the Bubble Act, the latter was repealed. In the Act of 1825 incorporation was made easier, while "unincorporated companies were left to the common law." [38] After the enactment of the Trade Companies Act of 1834 it became legally possible to create associations which according to common law were neither partnerships nor corporations, but had the possibility of suing or being sued through their offices. The Act of 1837 involved a still further extension and continued the first regulation concerning limited liability on shares. We do not need to go any farther here into the historical growth of joint-stock companies, for it should be clear from what has been said that achievement of the legal status by these companies in manufacture was relatively slow. They existed and began to play a considerable role in the financial structure of the de-

[34] Scott, *The Constitution and Finance of English, Scottish and Irish Joint-Stock Companies to 1720;* for the time after 1720 see Cunningham, *The Growth of English Industry and Commerce in Modern Times,* especially pp. 816 ff.

[35] Hansard, *Parliamentary Debates,* 1825, XIII, 1010.

[36] An excellent account of this process is given in H. A. Shannon, "The Coming of General Limited Liability," in *Economic History,* II (Jan., 1931), 267-291.

[37] *Ibid.,* p. 269.   [38] *Ibid.,* p. 276.

veloping industry before legal recognition had been granted. The very fact of their gradual emergence manifested a changing financial structure of industrial production. The new means of providing the capital needed by growing enterprise found its complementary expression in the changing form of the financial institutions which were wedded to the mode of production and therefore had to change with it.

Joint-stock banking would have been the natural outcome of the growth of industrial and commercial finance in the country at an earlier date if it had not been for the restrictions imposed upon the structure of banking through the Act of 1708. The financial crisis of December, 1825, brought home the fact that the inadequate banking structure of England [39] was responsible for the lack of banking control and financial integration which seemed to have been to a large extent responsible for the alleged overissue of paper. Such a presentation, however, seems to be an unwarranted oversimplification of the actual situation. While lack of integration in the banking structure cannot be denied, the source and the incentive for speculation did not lie with the financial institutions themselves, but was an inherent and unavoidable characteristic of the growing industrial production.[40] The latter made for ever-increasing demands for funds, and it was in compliance with these demands that the government had decided in 1822 to continue to permit the issue of country bank notes of less than £5 for another ten years. This, in accordance with the plan for the final and complete resumption of cash pay-

[39] By inadequate banking structure we refer to the existing country bank system with the restrictions on its growth and the unwillingness on the part of the Bank of England to extend its business over the whole country.

[40] Gregory (*The Westminster Bank through a Century,* I, 4) describes the surface phenomena of this process when he says that "Economic expansion involves a growth in the *scale* of the demands for accommodation with which the banker is confronted, and there arise difficult technical questions of spreading the risk adequately, as well as others concerning the liquidity of the loans granted when a setback occurs in economic conditions. The rhythm of economic life itself involves changes in the short-term trend of prices, but when such price changes are superimposed upon a changing long-term price trend, the strain upon the banking system is increased, and if the structure of the banking system is not *adequate* [italics ours] even to the normal demands made upon it, its operation must then prove extremely defective."

ments, should have been discontinued in 1823. These notes, particularly the £1 notes, had wide circulation as a means of paying wages, and the lack of regulation of their issue constituted in the opinion of a large part of the public a grave danger of overissue.

At the same time the Bank of England began to enter actively into the competition for the discounting of bills by reducing its rate of 4 percent and prolonging the run for bills eligible for discount from 65 to 95 days.

The speculative character of the accommodated demands for funds which, we maintain, was a necessary sign of that time, and the inadequate structure of the financial institutions providing these funds made themselves felt in 1825. The refusal of the Bank of England to continue to discount as a means of averting disaster turned out to accelerate disaster, and only through an equally sudden expansion of the Bank's volume of discount did it succeed in avoiding an even more formidable financial collapse.

Thomas Joplin probably comes nearest to the truth when he says that

the immediate cause of these difficulties was not then . . . generally understood. They were commonly attributed to overtrading, and wild speculations, the scarcity of money which existed was imputed to vast amounts supposed to be sunk in visionary undertakings, and the discredit and want of confidence it was presumed would merely extend to those houses who were implicated in them.[41]

Joplin is of the opinion that the panic could have been avoided if the Bank of England had not refused at first to give the necessary accommodation. "Can we be surprised that men would not part with their money, when the Bank dared not?" [42] He felt that it was for this reason that the disaster spread.

The policy of the Bank offers an interesting lesson in monetary policy. The type of reasoning employed by the directors

[41] Joplin, *An Examination of the Report of the Joint-Stock Bank Committee*, p. 70.
[42] *Ibid.*, pp. 70–71.

of the Bank and the advocates of the Bank's policy had become strangely divorced from the reality of the economic process. We find here the first formulation of those arguments with which we are so familiar in our own days and which at that time were not any more correct than they are today. It is here that we observe, if not the first, at least one of the early cases in which money was regarded as being imbued with a magic power which was supposed to be capable of adjusting and regulating the process of production according to the way in which money was consciously managed. Overissue was regarded as the definite cause of all evil, and the immediate restriction of credits and discounts was thought to be the efficient way out. Fortunately, the directors of the Bank were at that time largely still active business men themselves, not mere managers, and they were ready to correct their wrong reasoning and to salvage what still could be saved by reversing entirely their previous policy if only to save their own investments and profits. We shall return to this argument when we discuss the theory of deflation proper.

The one immediate result of the experience of 1825 was the recognition that the structure of the existing banking system had to be adapted to the new conditions. The great number of small country banks, each of which could have only local knowledge and experience and most of which were unable to provide for adequate reserves, were regarded as a positive danger. The lengthy discussions between the Government and the Bank of England, which had begun in 1822—materialized now in the Banking Copartnership Act of May, 1826 (7, Geo. IV, c. 46), legalizing the establishment of joint-stock banks outside a 65-mile radius of London, making it thus possible for country banks to be adequately provided with capital. The directors of the Bank of England were persuaded not to offer opposition to this concession by a provision for legal status for branches of the Bank of England to be established in the country.[43] At the same time, many of the London

[43] For a very full presentation of the negotiations between the Government and the Bank of England, as well as of the process of getting the respective

bankers discontinued the rediscounting of country bills, thus leaving this branch of the financial business entirely to the bill-brokers.

The permission to establish joint-stock banks, however, did not change the banking structure of England over night. The private country banks still continued their business, in which thereafter they had to compete with the rapidly developing joint-stock banks. The 65-mile radius around London in which no joint-stock banks were allowed to operate tended to give additional force to the need for continuation of localized banking even for the joint-stock banks, despite the impediments caused by the gradually growing net of transportation and the reinforced tendency of industry to concentrate in certain geographical areas.[44]

As we have seen, private banking originally developed because of the need to increase the available amount of currency by issuing notes. With the increasing integration of industrial society, the importance of note issue began to decline; though there began to develop the need for institutions where temporary funds could be kept remuneratively. This development toward deposit banking had previously created in Scotland and also in Ireland the establishment of the so-called "cash-credit" system. Though the Act of 1826 restricted the joint-stock banks by limiting the issue of demand notes and bills to places outside the 65-mile radius and bills on London to not less than £50 and at not less than six-month sight, the newly created joint-stock banks quickly realized their possibilities in the provinces and began an intense competition for all the available deposits. As the joint-stock banks could not establish banks or headquarters in London, they needed representatives for disposing of the funds collected in this manner, and the bill-brokers began to serve this function. Putting the development into its proper setting, it can easily be

---

laws formulated and sanctioned by Parliament see Gregory, *The Westminster Bank through a Century*, pp. 9 ff.

[44] Birnie, "The Growth of Industry in Europe from the Late Middle Ages to the Present Day," in *European Civilization*, ed. by Edward Eyre, pp. 312 ff.

deduced that it was the competition between the joint-stock banks and the private bankers, and even more so between the joint-stock banks themselves, that led to the discounting and, after the endorsement of the joint-stock banks, the rediscounting of paper whose questionable quality or even open speculative character would otherwise have prevented its coming into circulation. However, it should be emphasized again that speculation at that time, loaded as it was with potential dangers, was at the same time the very tool by means of which industrial society was gradually establishing itself.

The growth of joint-stock banking was astonishing. While in the beginning the note-issue privilege was retained, the banks established after 1828 concentrated on deposit banking. By 1839 nineteen joint-stock banks were in existence, and when, in 1833, nonissuing joint-stock banks were legalized in London, the formation of joint-stock banks began a mushroom development.[45] By 1840, 87 joint-stock banks had been established in England and Wales.[46] The official investigations of the parliamentary committees of 1832 and 1836 prove amply that the business of the joint-stock banks consisted predominantly of rediscounting through London.

One interesting point in the development of joint-stock banking is the apparent reversal of the direction of the business as compared with the original bill-broking with the private banks. Richardson had conceived of his business of bill-broking as sending bills from London to the country bank of Gurnell. The joint-stock banks as banks of deposit did just the opposite. They collected the available paper in the country and sent it to London for rediscount. The structural change underlying this reversal of the flow of bills can easily be understood if we remember that the ready cash which the country bank of Gurnell wanted to employ had originated predominantly in foreign trade, whereas the bills

---

[45] See the evidence, especially of Gurnell, before the Secret Committee on Joint Stock Banks on the Operation of Act 7, Geo. IV c. 46, permitting the establishment of Joint Stock Banks, *British Parliamentary Papers*, 1836 (591) 411.

[46] Thomas, *Rise and Growth of Joint Stock Banking*.

discounted for this cash were bills sent by the provincial country banks to procure cash for industrial transactions. The joint-stock banks operated to a considerable extent in the industrial centers, as the competitors or successors of the latter type of provincial country banks, and the ever-increasing demand for new circulating as well as fixed capital in industry provided them with a continuous source of bills to be discounted in London. The source of cash in London, on the other hand, was still provided by the London bankers, the Bank of England, and finally, and not the least important, by the merchants and the agricultural aristocracy.

It should be noted that this immediate give and take could continue only as long as the funds needed by industry and commerce were generally and relatively still scarce. To the degree, however, that the bank system succeeded in forming an integrated entity, the urgency in the demand for capital necessarily decreased, the more so as many of the smaller demands made upon the London market were again gradually being taken care of in the provinces themselves. The result was that the rediscounting provincial banks were willing to leave with the brokerage houses for very short periods the values thus credited to them through the rediscounting operations. The brokerage houses, on the other hand, were in greater need of such short-term funds as their business increased. It is in this way that the London "call" money market developed as the values resulting from the rediscounts were left with the brokerage houses till they were "called."

SAVINGS BANKS The gradual emancipation of labor, and accordingly the elimination of the responsibilities of the patriarchal landlords, had given rise in the last half of the eighteenth century to the formation of "Friendly Societies." Their main purpose was to create institutions of self-help among occupational classes to care for the expenses incidental to sickness and death. Under the Act of 1793 [47] encouragement had been given to these societies to raise "separate funds for

[47] 33, Geo. III. c. 54.

the mutual relief and the maintenance of the . . . members in sickness, old age and infirmity." To perform their function the societies had to build up reserve funds, and the increasing needs of industry offered a temptation to invest the funds in industrial enterprise rather than in government securities. The need of the emancipated classes for saving, as well as the need of the small traders, handicraft men, and even manufacturers to set apart some of their earnings for the purpose of later direct investments in industry and trade, soon created other institutions, which in the beginning were similar to the Friendly Societies. These became known as savings banks and were acknowledged under the Savings Bank Act of 1817.[48] Because of the lamentable state of its finances, the government took care to demand that all savings deposits exceeding £50 had to be remitted to the Office for the Reduction of the National Debt.[49] The economic importance of this provision compelling the savings banks to deposit their funds with the government cannot be underestimated. The savings banks, even more than the Friendly Societies, served the purpose of accumulating small and, because of their individual smallness, uninvestible funds. This, however, was only their direct function. Indirectly they made it possible to use the funds for industrial purposes after they had been collected. The size of these capital collecting agencies grew rapidly. In 1832 there were 408 trustee savings banks in England and Wales with 425,000 depositors and deposits of £40,332,000.[50]

Small as the savings banks were at the time under consideration, the fact that an institution was available in which the less monied groups of the population could deposit their small cash accumulations tended to influence in some quantitatively unaccountable amount the total volume of notes in circulation. Joplin recognized, at least in passing, this fact when in discussing the effects of country-bank failures he remarked that the proportion of notes "which is held by the

[48] 57, Geo. III. c. 130.

[49] Clapham, *An Economic History of Modern Britain; the Early Railway Age, 1820–1850*, I, 299.

[50] *Dictionary of Political Economy.*

lower classes [51] . . . can never be considerable, more especially since the Saving's Banks were established." [52]

CLEARINGHOUSES   Finally, there is to be considered the development and considerable growth of clearing establishments. Samuel Turner once said that in estimating the volume
and function of bank notes

a great mistake . . . arises from not having sufficiently considered
that Bank of England notes, at the present moment, do little more
than carry on the minor interchange of commodities between man
and man, and that, through the universal system of Banking, all
great changes of property, particularly in the metropolis, are effectuated almost without their aid, by means of mere book-transfers,
and that Bank-notes settle merely the little differences arising from
a multiplicity of transactions which are not precisely balanced.
. . . By the system of the clearing-house, the whole of the bankers
of London become almost as one bank, and we have it in evidence,
before the Bullion Committee, that about £220,000 in Bank-notes
are sufficient to settle the balance arising from the interchange of
drafts to the extent of £4,700,000. [53]

There are many legends about the origin of clearing. It is
known that by 1775 the clerks of the city banks in London
began to meet regularly in a room in Change Alley in order
to exchange the checks and drafts drawn upon the different
city banks. It was not until 1805 that larger quarters were
needed, and the earliest record we have of definite rules by a
Committee of Clearing Bankers supervising the clearing is
dated as of March 28, 1821. [54] There are no statistics available
as to the volume of checks and drafts cleared through this
institution before 1868. We may, however, infer from the development of deposit banking, to which we have referred, and
the increase in the use of checks, as well as from references of
the kind quoted above that the volume of clearing increased
considerably after 1805.

[51] We may read this to mean what would now be called "middle classes."
[52] Joplin, *An Essay on the General Principles and Present Practice of Banking in England and Scotland*, pp. 34–35.
[53] Turner, *A Letter Addressed to the Right Hon. Robert Peel*, pp. 51–52.
[54] Matthews, *The Bankers' Clearing House*, pp. 8 ff.

This increase in the volume of clearings necessarily affected the volume of bank notes and coins in circulation. Not only did it become unnecessary to send the clerks of the different city banks from one bank to another paying and collecting the amounts for checks and drafts drawn in cash, necessitating thus the use of large sums of money, but the clearing, once instituted, tended in itself to induce a larger use of checks and similar payments.

The effects of the operations of the clearinghouses were, however, not confined to city banks. The country banks participated to a limited extent at least in this institution through their London agent as long as the London agents were members of the clearinghouse.[55]

[55] Easton, *Money Exchange and Banking*, pp. 187 ff.

8 · The Theory of Deflation

Nominibus mollier licet mala

SINCE the wars were ended and the extraordinary military payments had ceased, the premium on bullion began to fall, first in 1814 and again after the final defeat of Napoleon at Waterloo. In the Act of 1816 initial preparations were made for the resumption of cash payments. In that year the price of gold fell to approximately its mint price. The Bank of England bought gold at the current market price and, after having coined it at a loss, began early in 1817 to redeem the notes below £5 in cash. It was permitted to do this under the regulations of the Restriction Act of 1797. In 1816 silver coins were reduced to the status of an auxiliary currency, and in 1819 the time-honored and often-evaded restrictions on the export of coin and bullion were repealed. The process of the gradual formation of a legal basis for a gold standard had thus reached the goal. The Act of 1819 repealed the Restriction Act of 1797 and provided for the redemption of notes in gold bars, a provision which was changed in 1821, when the Bank was allowed to pay its notes in bullion or coin.

Immediately after these steps had been taken, the exchanges began to fall in favor of England. At the same time, the prices of commodities exhibited a noticeable tendency to decline.

CHARACTER OF THE FALL OF THE GENERAL PRICE LEVEL   In explaining the rise in the general price level during the period of the Anglo-French wars, it can be argued that the rise had been due to the extraordinary credits which the government had been forced to take out in order to finance the war and the equally extraordinary remittances to foreign countries in order to pay either directly for the expenses of the English armies or indirectly to subsidize those nations which were fighting the cause of the English commercial interests. Nationally, however, the increase in prices has to be explained primarily with reference to the type of productive expansion whose very character it was to proceed irregularly and in the form of speculation.

The essence of the change of the economic and financial structure as it existed in and after 1815 consisted of a gradual but definite smoothing out of the ups and downs which had been so characteristic of the earlier period. This process of gradual integration of the industrial mode of production was accompanied by a growth of financial institutions which were increasingly capable of taking care of the financial needs, and a development of the means of transportation and communication to such a degree of efficiency that some of the most inhibitive barriers between the different economic regions as well as between the provinces and London began to disappear.

It is only too obvious that such developments cannot possibly be explained in exact quantitative terms. It is only a knowledge of the degree of integration of an economic system which allows us to understand and to evaluate the relative importance of price-level changes. Because of the lack of integration and the relatively slow development of the productive forces, David Hume, as well as Adam Smith, was still little interested in the changes of the general price level. What they had been talking about when they maintained that any change in the volume of money would immediately be reflected in the prices was the price level of imported commodities. Coupled with this was the fact that production for home consumption as well as home consumption itself were still relatively undeveloped. In the theory of inflation of the first stage of the bullion controversy considerable attention was focused upon the problem of maladjustments in prices conceived as resulting from monetary policies. The theorizing at this stage was predominantly based upon unwarranted identification of prices in international trade and provincial prices, relating either to commodities used in production or to finished products. It was only after 1815 that the integration of the economic system of the provinces with that of London was developed far enough to allow for a relatively immediate sensitivity of the prices between these economic spheres.

It may be mentioned here in passing that another fundamental condition had to be fulfilled in order to make such direct interdependence possible—the process of expansion must be allowed to proceed without being hindered by rigidities and limitations created in its own development. We have in mind here the later emergence of industrial monopolies, price cartels, and the type of difficulty in international trade which was first experienced, to a noticeable extent, after the 1870's, and in a later phase of which we are today. In the stage of the development of industrial society under consideration these characteristics did not yet exist, and therefore they could not possibly be included in the theories.

RECURRENCE OF THE DOCTRINE OF FORCED SAVINGS   Numerous attempts were made during this period to explain the peculiar movements of the price level and to provide a logical framework upon which it would be possible to build an adequate and workable monetary policy to be followed uniformly by those institutions entrusted with the direction of the flow of money. Thomas Attwood explained the opinion generally held, based upon the theories developed by Hume and Smith, that any sudden and general fall in the prices of all commodities would not have injurious or beneficial reactions to any considerable degree as long as "the amount of debts and obligations were to fall in the same proportion, at the same time." [1] He pointed out, on the other hand, that the greatest obstacle, as well as injury, was produced by the relative fixity of the cost of production. Here we have one of those important differences in theory to which we have referred above. As long as the trade function was predominant in English economy, changes in the price level affected commodities to be sold as well as those to be bought. Industrial society, however, was dependent upon the factors of production, among which, as far as immediate outlays were concerned, labor cost still played a dominant role. Attwood argued that the process of adjustment would be rather lengthy and injurious, since falling

[1] Thomas Attwood, *Prosperity restored,* p. 78.

prices and stable labor costs would force employers to dismiss labor and find themselves able to re-employ only after labor was willing to work for lower wages in accordance with the fall in the price level. In these arguments the same position was taken regarding the function of capital. The idea that more capital equaled more production implied that the less capital there was, the less production there would be.

These, among others, according to Mathias Attwood, are "those ulterior principles by which supply and demand are themselves governed '*upon which* a lessened quantity of money *is operating* in reducing prices.' " [2] There is no indication that the Attwoods argued "a dependence of the 'demand and supply' of price theory on the state of currency." [3] The difference between the Attwoods and Ricardo lies in the fact that the former were interested in the short-run movements, while the latter was primarily concerned with a structural analysis. Both these attitudes were, however, still founded upon a predominant interest in production, not distribution, that is, prices. The point, therefore, was not that Attwood argued that "an increase in the quantity of money will . . . not decrease [output]," [4] but that a decrease in the quantity of money *will* decrease output, though this decrease of output will begin with "an abundance of goods." Similarly, Thomas Attwood does not argue (against Sir Henry Parnell) [5] that the conditions of the supply of commodities should be neglected, but "that there are two sides of the question," namely, "that the 'market price of commodities' depends just as much upon 'the proportion' between the supply of, and the demand for *money,* as it does upon 'the proportion' between the supply of and the demand for *commodities.*" [6] Attwood attacked Parnell only for having neglected entirely the one side, namely, "the reference to the state of currency," but he himself does not disregard entirely the "obscure, uncontrol-

[2] Mathias Attwood, *A Letter to Lord Archibald Hamilton on Alterations in the Value of Money,* pp. 48–49.

[3] Viner, *Studies in the Theory of International Trade,* p. 199.

[4] *Ibid.,* p. 199n.

[5] Parnell, *Observations on Paper Money, Banking and Overtrading,* p. 40.

[6] Thomas Attwood, *The Scotch Banker,* p. 70.

lable, and capricious principles," which act upon "the supply of, and demand for commodities." His fundamental concern is still *production: "dear money* and *low* prices . . . strangled the industry of the country by compelling it to discharge monied obligations which its monied prices will not redeem." [7]

It is because of the danger to production, caused by decreased capital supply as a result of the contraction in the volume of currency, that the problem of forced savings comes to the foreground. Joplin formulated this doctrine for the first time with a certain degree of comprehension. Thornton, Malthus, and the others were predominantly concerned with the effects of a rise in prices upon the economic structure. Joplin said:

if a person pays a thousand pounds into the hands of a banker, and the currency is contracted to that extent, both one thousand pounds of capital and one thousand pounds of currency are destroyed. The commodities represented by the money thus *saved* [italics ours] and cancelled, are thrown on the market, prices are reduced, and the power of consuming them is obtained by the holders of the money left in circulation.[8]

Thus we are concerned here with quite a different type of forced savings from the one considered by Bentham, Malthus, and Thornton. The latter were concerned primarily with the added value created by indirect saving, and they had voiced only moral condemnation of the social effects resulting from such an accumulation of capital, which was "involuntary" only as far as the workers were concerned. Joplin now points to a case in which involuntary saving was suffered by the industrial producers and the farmers, and to them this case was much more serious.[9] It follows, therefore, quite logically from

[7] *Ibid.,* p. 71.

[8] *An Illustration of Mr. Joplin's Views on Currency,* 1825, p. 28, cited by Viner, in *Studies in the Theory of International Trade,* pp. 190–191.

[9] We do not agree that Bentham held the same views as Joplin. It is perfectly true that the sentence of Mr. Bentham, in which he states that because of the forced saving, the "national wealth is increased" continues "at the expense of national comfort and national justice" (*Works,* III, 45). But the emphasis in the whole of the reasoning of Bentham as well as that of

the general position on the basis of which Joplin argues that he cannot approve of forced savings.[10] Then the theory was formulated that investment should equal voluntary savings. On this basis it was clear that the occurrence of the deflation was viewed with great concern, which latter resulted in Joplin's proposals for a banking reform. How, then, was it supposed to be possible to devise a means not only to counteract inflation but also to guarantee that deflation would not occur again?

THE CHANGING FUNCTION OF INTEREST   Joplin suggested that no involuntary saving would take place if a rate of interest could be charged which would keep savings and borrowings equal. "Whether it ought to be three, four, or five percent can only be determined by the proportion which the supply of the savings of income bears to the demand in the market." [11] The procedure thus proposed consisted of a flexible rate of interest. Interest "can no more be fixed at any particular rate than the price of sugar, coffee, or any other commodity." [12]

Even the Bank of England acted according to this principle: "for, though it fixes a particular rate in dealing with the public, it can never . . . keep its advances steady at that rate: and it is frequently obliged to take less, by purchasing exchequer bills or otherwise." [13] For this purpose, however, Joplin saw the need for a stable currency which would force the banks to lend out in credit or currency only what had

---

Thornton seems to be placed upon the increase of the national wealth rather than upon concern for the national comfort and national justice. If we want to look for an economic reason why men like Bentham and Thornton were at all concerned with the latter, it may be found in the fact that they were as yet little concerned with production and that they looked upon the advantages to production in the same way that they looked upon the disadvantages to labor. There is no place to our knowledge in either Bentham's or Thornton's writings in which either one of them discusses the disadvantages to be suffered by the holders of capital from the effects of forced savings.

[10] Joplin, *Views on the Currency in Which the Connexion Between Corn and Currency is Shown*, 1828, pp. 35–37.

[11] Joplin, *Views on the Corn Bill of 1827 and Other Measures of Government*, p. 151.

[12] *Ibid.*   [13] *Ibid.*, pp. 151–152.

previously been saved. The volume of money "ought if possible, to be . . . fixed." [14] This statement in connection with
the function of the interest rate is of considerable importance,
since it avowedly disregards the expansive character of the
contemporary industrial economy. Here we have one of the
important statements constructed on the assumption of a
static economy, which did not coincide with the quasi-static
character which that economy was exhibiting. Joplin over-
steps his point by insisting upon a quantitatively fixed volume
of money. If such a policy had been followed, the interest rate
would soon have been increased to the level of the profit rate,
strangling, thus, all possible incentive for investment and
emphasizing exactly those circumstances about which he was
quite correctly concerned.

As far as the statement concerning the function of the rate
of interest is concerned, he carried it one step farther than
the argument of Henry Thornton.[15] Thornton had already
pointed out that the desirable volume of credit could be determined by "a comparison of the rate of interest taken at the
Bank with the current rate of mercantile profit." The emphasis here is, however, still on mercantile profit. It is again only
Joplin who realizes that it is rather the industrial profit which
would be relevant to the volume of money advanced. That
the interest rate could effectively function as a check to the
amount of money to be brought into circulation presupposed,
however, a general economic condition which was characterized by a satisfactory supply of capital to the developing industry before such a check would come into operation. This
condition existed only with regard to merchant capital in the
period from David Hume to Henry Thornton—and so far
they were correct. Only after 1815 had the integration of industrial production and the creation of an adequate financial
structure developed far enough to provide gradually the same
opportunities to industry that had earlier existed for trade.

[14] *Ibid.*, p. 37.
[15] Thornton, *An Enquiry into the Nature and Effects of the Paper Credit
of Great Britain*, p. 287.

The subject matter, therefore, which Thornton treated was in content dialectically opposed to the subject matter which Joplin was treating. This change in content, hidden behind the apparent continuity of doctrine, offers another example of the dangers with which we play when we argue on the basis of pure doctrine.

VOLUME AND VALUE OF MONEY   Ricardo stated that if his plan were to be followed the fall in prices would be equal to the prevailing premium on gold. When prices fell from 198 in 1814 to 135 in 1816 and to 124 in 1820, that is, by nearly 32 percent in 1816 and by 38 percent in 1820, the average annual percentage deviations from the par of Spanish silver dollars was 26.4 in 1814, 2.3 in 1816, and 1.5 in 1820.[16] According to the Ricardian type of computation the currency was then deflated by somewhat more than 13 percent in 1820.

Professor Silberling has computed that the total advances of the Bank of England between 1814 and 1820 decreased by over 48 percent.[17] The latter figure was perhaps counterbalanced to some extent by the note issues of, and credit expansion through, the country banks.[18]

Beyond this the Bank had violated the plan, drawn up by Ricardo and incorporated into the Bill by Peel, by beginning immediately to accumulate bullion through purchases at the price of £3.17.10½.[19] Large amounts of this gold were paid for in goods exported by industry and trade when both the latter were actively and successfully engaged in regaining and progressing beyond the scope of the trade domain which they

[16] Silberling, "Financial and Monetary Policy of Great Britain during the Napoleonic Wars," *Quarterly Journal of Economics*, XXXVIII, 225.

[17] Silberling, "British Prices and Business Cycles 1779–1850," *Review of Economic Statistics*, Vol. V, Supplement, 1923, p. 255. Professor Silberling gives quarterly figures. We use in the following simple yearly averages.

[18] As Dr. Viner has pointed out, the indices of Silberling for the country note circulation based upon the aggregate sales of stamps, and then arbitrarily multiplied by ten, cannot serve as an adequate means for the determination of the actual volume of country notes effective, as they do not take care of the amounts of old notes going out of circulation within that period nor of the amount of old notes used over again (Viner, *Studies in the Theory of International Trade*, pp. 163–165).

[19] Ricardo, *Works*, ed. by McCulloch, p. 469.

had held before the wars, especially before the Continental Blockade. It was maintained that this all-too-ready demand for gold abroad had raised the exchanges in favor of England, with the result that the value of money in terms of gold began to fall. The Bank had not only accumulated large quantities of bullion but also had begun to coin money, in consequence of which it was "absolutely forced to come to the legislature for promises last year to pay in specie." [20] It is mainly this "mismanagement" of the Bank which was blamed by Ricardo for the rise in the value of money beyond the 5 percent anticipated by him on the basis of the divergence of the exchange rates from the mint price.

Ricardo stood more or less alone during this time in upholding the correctness of the resumption of cash payments. Peel's bill was increasingly attacked in Parliament and in public because of the consequent fall in prices. Cobbett was one of the leaders of the attack against the resumption of cash payments and its supposed results. He maintained that, not gold, but corn was "the only fair standard." "This queer, this 'Change Alley' . . . notion of the price of gold being the standard" was to him the real danger.[21] Cobbett shows here some considerable insight into the character of a monetary standard which he might well and effectively have used against some of the arguments that he himself and others brought forward against Ricardo. In Cobbett's argument against Ricardo, however, the reference to the "functional" character of a monetary standard was beside the point. Cobbett was definitely wrong when he imagined that corn could fulfill the position of a functional or "true" monetary standard under the existing conditions. As Ricardo had maintained that the fluctuations of the standard which had increased the value of money were due to mismanagement and to the deviation from his original plan, he was perfectly correct in regarding

[20] Ricardo to McCulloch, 3d of January, 1822, *Letters of Ricardo to McCulloch*, p. 120.

[21] Cobbett, *Weekly Political Register*, October 20, 1821, pp. 925–926; see also *Letters of David Ricardo to Hutches Trower and Others*, ed. by James Bonar and J. H. Hollander, p. 169.

Cobbett's objections as irrelevant. "He shews his [Cobbett's] ignorance . . . in saying so, but supposing it true, can he tell me what is to secure us from variations in his standard,— it would perhaps be more variable than any other." [22]

Ricardo's whole argument in explanation of the deflation of prices was still based upon the axioms that the premium on bullion was *the* measure for the inflation caused by the suspension of the cash payments. No index numbers existed in Ricardo's time, aside from calculations such as those of Tooke, who had estimated a rise in the value of currency of about 5 percent, with which Ricardo agreed.[23] Ricardo, therefore, can have had only "a vague idea as to the extent of the fall in the price level which had occurred, and he seems to have seriously underestimated it." [24] This mere underestimation cannot explain fully, however, the rigid adherence of Ricardo to his explanation of the previous inflation in analyzing the succeeding deflation. Ricardo neglected entirely to take into account the change in the structure of production to which we have referred. It is at this point that Cobbett's criticism of the notion of a monetary standard became valid (though the validity is rather implied than argued). We find here a first, and as such hardly recognizable, sign of purely theoretical reasoning. By "purely" we mean a reasoning the basic assumptions of which are no longer founded in the reality which they purport to explain.[25] In the analysis of the inflationary phase of the monetary development of England around the turn of the eighteenth century, Ricardo had led the discussion on the causes of the rise of prices to a plane on which this rise was quite correctly designated as a deviation from the "normal" trend in the value of money. Now, when the prices of commodities began to fall, Ricardo explained this fall by giving opposite values to the same arguments he had used for the explanation of the inflation.

---

[22] *Letters of David Ricardo to Hutches Trower,* p. 169.

[23] *The Works of David Ricardo,* p. 471.

[24] Viner, *Studies in the Theory of International Trade,* p. 175.

[25] See the remarks concerning this point in the "Methodological Introduction."

Samuel Turner, an ex-director of the Bank of England and a pamphleteer in the latter's behalf, was conscious of the most important argument to be made against the reasoning of Ricardo, though his previous position as director of the Bank of England seems to have prevented him from coming to those conclusions which were actually implied in his arguments.[26] He reasoned that during the period of the wars the volume of the medium of exchange had had to increase. While he does not include in his argument the causes which prevented the international exchange from readjusting the price level— the payments of the English treasury for the war operations abroad were necessarily exhaustive—he concluded quite correctly that their cessation had to have deflationary results. More important, however, is the fact that he added to this argument that

It will not be denied, for the history of this and of every other country will prove the fact, that as society improves . . . wealth becomes more abundant (and by wealth I do not mean merely an increase in the precious metals, but an increase in the produce of the lands and labour of a country, and augmentation of its fixed capital, buildings, live and dead stock).[27]

If the volume of money in relation to the volume of commodities is reduced, prices must fall, but "if prices are reduced, contracts could not be fulfilled . . . What, therefore, is the remedy by which society is still kept together, and different articles still bear their relative value one toward another? I answer, an increase of the circulating medium." [28] We do not wish to go minutely into the arguments of Turner nor to follow his acrobatics in turning this reasoning into conclusions fundamentally opposed to his own initial argument.[29]

[26] Samuel Turner had ceased to be a director of the Bank of England at the time of the resumption of cash payments in 1819; see Turner, *A Letter Addressed to the Right Hon. Robert Peel*, p. 81; see also *Studies in the Theory of International Trade*, Viner, p. 181.

[27] *Ibid.*, pp. 13–14.   [28] *Ibid.*, pp. 16, 18.

[29] Turner argued that an increase in taxes because of an increase in expenditures amounted to a decrease in the volume of circulation. This argument, as it stands, was validly attacked by Ricardo (see Ricardo, "On Protection of Agriculture," in *The Works of David Ricardo*, 4th edition, London,

While Ricardo had neglected this phenomenon of increasing "wealth," that is, of an expanded economy, regarding it very likely as irrelevant to the problem in question, his reasoning was of little practical harm to the economic development.[30] Ricardo made it quite clear that what he was after was not a rigid gold standard, with gold coins circulating as the medium of exchange, but a gold bullion standard, with gold merely as a reserve for contingencies.

If that plan had been adopted, not a particle of gold would have been used in the circulation,—all our money must have consisted of paper, excepting the silver coin necessary for payments under the value of a pound. In that case it is demonstrable, that the value of money could only have been raised 5 percent, by reverting to the fixed ancient standard, for that was the whole difference between the value of gold and paper.[31]

Once the directors of the Bank had decided to withdraw the paper below £5 and to issue gold coins instead, Ricardo argued that the premium on gold had to recur because of the necessary gold purchases. According to Tooke these gold purchases were made by the directors of the Bank of England, "only in the ordinary routine of their business: they bought gold simply as it was brought to them at or below the Mint price."[32] It is perfectly true that the premium on bullion had fallen in 1816 until the price was very near the Mint price for gold bullion; but it is equally true that immediately after the beginning of the purchases of gold abroad this premium be-

---

1882, p. 471) who pointed out that "if its pressure is felt by the tenant it must be advantageous to the landlord and to the receivers of taxes." However, what both neglect to consider is that a large amount of the government expenditures during the wars were, as we have said, of an exhaustive kind.

Turner advocated the withdrawal of all £1 and £2 notes of the Bank of England and their payment in gold and silver coins (3d paragraph of "Resolutions," in *A Letter Addressed to the Right Hon. Robert Peel*, p. 87).

[30] Ricardo, "Letter to the Morning Chronicle," September 18, 1810, in *Minor Papers on the Currency Question, 1809–1823*, ed. by J. H. Hollander, p. 74.

[31] Ricardo, *Works*, p. 468.

[32] Thomas Tooke, *A History of Prices and of the State of the Circulation from 1792 to 1856*, II, 108n.

gan to rise again. While the average annual percentage deviation from the par of Spanish silver dollars in 1816 had been
2.3, it was 5.4 in 1817 and 11.6 in 1818. Though these figures
may not be entirely conclusive, they do offer strong evidence
in support of Ricardo's argument that there was some relation
between the gold purchases and the premium on bullion.
Tooke had continued his argument by saying that "it was a
matter of indifference, as concerned the amount of the currency, whether the gold were taken by the importers to the
Mint, and thence brought directly into circulation as coin,
or were taken in the shape of bullion to the Bank in return
for its notes." [33] This statement is logical as long as it stands
by itself. In the specific context in which it is used, however,
it is wrong. The bringing of gold to the Mint for coinage
presupposed, first of all, that the gold was already acquired
from abroad, just the fact which Ricardo complained about.
Secondly, Tooke's argument assumed that the public would
be wanting to exchange the notes in their hands for this gold.
This obviously could be true only under two conditions: (a)
if confidence in the currency were seriously disturbed and
people preferred hard money to paper, which, however, was
not anticipated by either Tooke or Ricardo; (b) people might
be willing to bring their notes to the Bank in exchange for
gold coins if they then could bring the gold coins to the Mint
and exchange them there against more Bank of England notes
than they had originally given to the Bank in exchange for
the bullion. While this second condition proved to be true, it
was explained by Ricardo as having been the result of the
premature gold purchases of the Bank of England at a price
increasingly above the Mint price, as there was admittedly no
reason for anticipating a special disturbance of the confidence
of the people in the currency.

The arguments put forward against Ricardo's reasoning
can thus be found not valid. Other arguments concerning the
results of speculative anticipations of a rise and fall, respectively, in the value of currency were properly ignored by

[33] *Ibid.*

Ricardo.[34] They could have, from his point of view as well as from ours, no valid relation to the more fundamental problem with which Ricardo was concerned.

If Ricardo is interpreted as having stated the basic reasons for the existing deflation, his argument is wrong. This deflation was of a structural nature caused by the increasing application of the machine, that is, labor-saving production. The general tendency toward deflation, little observed at the time, was accentuated further by the gradual, but by now definite, industrialization of the Continent. The attempt on the Continent to catch up with the economic development of England —a process which was not finished until the period between 1870 and 1914—inevitably resulted in an increasing scarcity of the precious metals. This was true of gold as well as of silver, even though most countries outside England were still nominally on a silver standard, or at least on a bimetallic standard with the emphasis on silver.

Later the successful avoiding of deflation will be considered. Ricardo's answer to this question was to leave the creation of capital alone, after having taken care that no interference could come from artificial causes external to the automatic working of the economic mechanics.

The supply of capital, according to Ricardo, was a function of the effective demand for commodities, limited only by possible use in ways which in turn would lower the profit rate and restrain the investment of capital. The invested capital itself originates from voluntary savings, since people are induced, because of the limitlessness of demand, not to consume the surplus they have above their consumptive needs, but to invest in production at a profit.[35]

This type of reasoning represents a classical mechanistic analysis.

[34] Woods, *Observations on the Present Price of Bullion and Rates of Exchange*, p. 9; Prentice, *Thoughts on the Repeal of the Bank Restriction Law*, p. 50, cited by Viner, *Studies in the Theory of International Trade*, p. 184. It has to be noted, however, that Woods as well as Prentice was actually concerned with the problem of inflation, not with deflation.

[35] Ricardo, "Principles of Political Economy and Taxation," in *Works*, pp. 174 ff.

It is not supposed [says Ricardo] that he [the pro
any length of time, be ill-informed of the com:
can most advantageously produce, to attain th
has in view, namely the possession of other goo
it is not probable that he will continually pro
for which there is no demand.[36]

Ricardo was quite right. At his time there was no reason
why the producer should continue in one line of production
when there was no demand for the product and at the same
time there were plenty of productive opportunities in other
lines. Certainly the volume of fixed capital, per enterprise as
well as for the whole of the English economy, had increased.
But at the same time we can notice that no general rigidities
had yet developed in the industrial structure of England. The
still relatively small degree of fixity of capital and the relatively low status of concentration and combination left ample
space for further expansion and provided equally well for the
possibility of actual change from one type of production to
another if and when the opportunity arose. We may add also
that the financial structure of industry, for example, the initial stage of joint-stock enterprise with its hardly existing
absentee ownership still made for an easy transfer of capital.
It held true, even if temporary losses and speculative anticipations had to be considered rather than certainties regarding
the forthcoming profits. This was because the responsibility
still rested with the owner-manager, or at least the predominant owner-manager, who was willing and able to take the
risk for himself.

On a basis of this reality and only on a basis of such reality,
was Ricardo correct in maintaining that every fluctuation in
the quantity and value of money is but of temporary duration.

If, by the discovery of a new mine, by the abuses of banking, or
by any other cause, the quantity of money be greatly increased,
its ultimate effect is to raise the prices of commodities in proportion to the increased quantity of money.[37]

36 *Ibid.*, pp. 174–175.
37 Ricardo, "Effects of Accumulations on Profits and Interest," in *Works,*
p. 179.

THE THEORY OF DEFLATION

can state, therefore, that the theoretical explanation practical conclusions offered by Ricardo expressed phenomenally the actual state of affairs. Or as we may put it now, Ricardo's theoretical procedure to *de facto,* presupposing an economic *statics,*[38] did not yet do violence to any concrete, observable economic event. At the same time, however, certain indications could be found of a gradual change in that institutional contemporary setting. In our paragraphs on the changed statics of the doctrine of forced savings and the changing function of interest we have already referred to some such institutional changes in the setting. A number of economists were mentioned who observed these phenomena without being able to integrate their observations into a consistent economic theory.

THE INTERRELATION OF CONSUMPTION AND PRODUCTION   An even more important institutional change is observable in the relation between consumption and production. We have referred to the historical fact that production in the first twenty years after the turn of the eighteenth century was increasing. The termination of the wars brought, necessarily, a shift in the consumptive demand, giving at least an additional impetus to the expansion of production.[39] The structural development of the English economy created a situation in which production began to outdistance consumption, or as we may more properly put it, in which consumption began to lag at least temporarily behind production. This situation was further emphasized by the necessary excesses of the inflationary period. This necessary speculative and anticipatory character of the expanding economy found its equally necessary counterpart in the constantly delayed catching-up of con-

[38] Professor Adolf Loewe, for example, says that "the whole classical analysis was based on the supposition that all movements in the market are nothing but short-run interruptions of a state of objective equilibrium, and therefore negligible if the fundamental order is to be studied. . . . Under classical assumptions this working rule (*ceteris paribus*) had a realistic significance—other things, in fact, remaining equal during the course of a mere short-run friction." Loewe, *Economics and Sociology,* p. 88.

[39] Malthus, *Principles of Political Economy,* pp. 331–334; also Ricardo, "Principles," in *Works,* p. 160.

sumption with production. The very character of industrial production, as we understand it, lay in the fact that the productive capacities among other things created the consumptive demand by transforming the soil-bound agricultural and luxury-goods-trading society into a wage-earning society, which became dependent upon industrial production to the extent of the development of that production.

At the same time, the remuneration, that is, the return in the form of commodities for labor used in the process of production, had to exhibit a tendency to decrease per time unit of labor rendered to the degree that power and machine production usurped a larger proportional share in the process of production. The already existing trend of consumption to lag behind production was thus emphasized by the growing decrease of labor cost per unit of production. It is granted that this trend was only periodically visible at that time and that because of the very nature of the expansion of industry the lagging consumption was actually able to catch up occasionally with production. This was possible because, while labor cost per unit of production decreased, the total volume of labor employed was still increasing enormously.

It is obvious, therefore, that according to an all-inclusive static theoretical approach, as Ricardo used it, this process of lagging and catching up could appear only as a series of deviations from a basically static equilibrium. This also can be seen from the complementary phenomenon that there were at the same time a number of economists who were little concerned with a logically necessary comprehensiveness and consistency in economic theory, but concentrated upon particular economic phenomena. These seemed to offer problems in the English economy, the immediate solution of which appeared to these economists to be mandatory, and because of the urgent demands of industry itself, they did not think they could be left to the gradual working out according to equilibrium principles. The increase in consumptive demand complementary to the continuing, though less urgent, growth of accumulation was such a problem.

Bentham had already tried to explain this phenomenon of lagging consumption. It is not surprising, in view of the rather noticeable taxation upon consumption, that Bentham argued that the revenues were taxed away from that part of the income which otherwise would have been used for consumptive purposes. Bentham came to the conclusion that if the revenues collected by the government were spent for productive purposes, the people who had been taxed would have to suffer a "forced frugality." [40] This same type of argument was carried on by Turner, though he treated it more technically.[41]

SAVINGS AND INVESTMENT   In mercantile times capital was tantamount to the ability to use bullion for trade and manufacturing purposes. The predominant purpose of wanting to dispose of bullion was to engage in the exchange of commodities.

In the period we have been concerned with here, capital constituted the power-to-dispose over the factors of production. By "factors of production" we mean machines and labor, the latter being at that time still of predominant importance. The important point for the process of industrial accumulation and its relation to saving is that the ability to use machines and labor already participating in the process of production presupposed an act of saving, that is, of setting aside part of the annual produce for these purposes. Concretely, it meant the production of these machines instead of consumers' goods and the production of only those consumers' goods necessary to obtain the labor of those employed in the process of production. Even if the process of production is expanding in volume, new groups of laborers, taken into production and out of their semi-serf status in agriculture, necessitated the acquisition of adequate food stuffs for them in agriculture and therewith again presupposed an act of saving.

The form in which this saving took place is important. In

[40] Bentham, "Manual of Political Economy," *Works*, III, 44.
[41] Turner, *A Letter Addressed to the Right Hon. Robert Peel . . . . ,* pp. 18 ff.

order not to fall into the usual confusion of language and
logic when we later present some of the theoretical expositions of this problem as it existed at that time, we shall have
to remember the aspects of the problem that the different
theoreticians had in mind. It was Ricardo's distinct opinion
that no investment could possibly be made which was not
based on saving. It is a virtue of Ricardo's theoretical reasoning that in this respect at least he tried to be as concrete as
possible.[42] "Credit," Ricardo said, "does not create capital;
it determines only by whom that capital should be employed."
And he continued that "capital can only be acquired by saving." [43] As Professor Viner has pointed out, Ricardo denied
that any excess issue can serve as a stimulus to production. It
cannot be emphasized too much that Ricardo's reasoning is
based on the assertion that demand is a function of production, not the reverse, as we find it maintained by the post-
classicists and the marginal utilitarians. We have already said
that Ricardo's theory exhibited definite signs of a static concept of the economic process, and it may be added that his
concept of production was also static. If Viner argues that
Ricardo's concepts of supply and demand were "too physical"
and contained "an implicit assumption of price and money—
cost flexibility too unrealistic," [44] we should like to refer to
our previous presentation of the type of economy in which
Ricardo was living. An outstanding characteristic of this society was its money cost flexibility, and this rather fundamental condition distinguishes that society not only from the
one with which Jevons and Böhm-Bawerk were concerned
but also, above all, from our own. It is only with reference to
our own contemporary economic reality that Viner's objections to a Ricardian interpretation could be sustained.

Also, the well-known argument of Malthus against John
Stuart Mill cannot be considered adequate. Mill had main-

[42] To the contrary, see Viner, *Studies in the Theory of International Trade,*
pp. 197–198.

[43] *Reports by the House of Lords, Secret Committee to Inquire into the
State of the Bank of England; with Reference to the Expediency of the
Resumption of Cash Payments,* pp. 192–193.

[44] *Cf.,* Viner, *Studies in the Theory of International Trade,* p. 198.

tained, as had Ricardo, that "a loan is a mere transfer of a portion of capital from the landlord to the government." [45] This assertion of Mill is again based upon the theory that demand and supply of capital must necessarily tend toward equality. The objection which Malthus raised against this position is somewhat amusing. First, he accuses Ricardo of using the term frequently "as if saving were an end instead of a means," whereas Ricardo had said: "Mr. Malthus never appears to remember that to save is to spend, as surely, as what he exclusively calls spending." [46] This, indeed, is the crux of the matter, because Malthus continues in the same paragraph, after having said that saving

can never be considered either immediately or permanently in any other light than as a means . . . [that] if however commodities are already so plentiful that an adequate portion of them is not profitably consumed, to save capital can only be still further to increase the plenty of commodities, and still further to lower already low profits, which can be comparatively of little use. [47]

Ricardo spoke of saving as an economic act, and of that he said, "I know no other way of saving, but saving from unproductive expenditure to add to productive expenditure." [48] He had definitely not spoken of hoarding, but it is of hoarding that Malthus is speaking, not of saving. Ricardo never denied the possibility that disproportional increase in the volume of money and the consequent rise in the prices of commodities could lead to temporary disturbances. [49] But these disturbances would be only temporary and as far as their effect upon accumulation was concerned, Ricardo agreed that a forced saving for the workers would follow. [50] As far as hoarding is concerned, Ricardo held with Torrens that

[45] *Westminster Review*, II (1823), 39 (John Stuart Mill's "Review of William Blake's 'Observations on the Effects Produced by the Expenditure of Government,'" 1823).

[46] Ricardo, *Notes on Malthus' Principles of Political Economy*, ed., J. H. Hollander and T. E. Gregory, 1925, p. 245.

[47] Malthus, *Principles of Political Economy*, p. 401.

[48] Ricardo, *Notes on Malthus' Principles of Political Economy*, p. 231.

[49] *Reports of the House of Lords Secret Committee*, pp. 198–199.

[50] It is not clear why Ricardo's statement "that the changed proportions"

with the exception of a few insane misers who hoard their treasures, all persons are desirous of consuming whatever wealth they can acquire, either productively with a view to improving their condition, or else unproductively, with a view to their immediate enjoyment. The alterations which occasionally take place in the distribution of industry, may lead to temporary embarrassment; but after the readjustment has been effected, and commodities are brought to market in quantities duly proportioned to each other, the increased supply will be accompanied by increased demand. . . . Increased production . . . provided it be general and duly proportioned is precisely the same thing as extended demand.[51]

This maze cannot possibly be made clear without keeping track of the actual points of departure of the reasoning put forward by the different theorists. Ricardo in all his arguments was concerned with elucidating the general behavior and the laws of the industrial economy. It is a manifestation of his very method that he could conceive of particular phenomena within the larger framework of the general rules of industrial production as a whole. Malthus also used generalizations, though they might be better described as "generalities." Consistency within a given system of approach was never his strength.[52] He loses sight, here, of the contradiction between the arguments from the particular to the general and from the general to the particular. If by "investment" we

---

in the division of the national income resulting from an excess note circulation "may facilitate the accumulation of capital in the hands of the capitalists; he having increased profits while the laborer has diminished wages" (Ricardo's evidence before the House of Lords' Secret Committee, 1819, pp. 198–200) is "not an acceptance of the forced saving doctrine" (Viner, *Studies in the Theory of International Trade*, p. 197). Viner maintains that "the increase of investment is held [by Ricardo] to result indirectly and voluntarily from the redistribution of income from a non-saving to a saving group, rather than directly and voluntarily from the consumer's cost of living" (*ibid.*). If the above quotation of Ricardo's has any meaning at all, especially in view of his theory of wages, it can only mean that the wages of the laborers are diminished directly by the rise in the consumer's cost of living and that is to all intents and purposes what is meant by forced saving.

[51] "Mr. Owen's Plan for Relieving the National Distress," *Edinburgh Review*, XXXII (October, 1819), 473. Ricardo was of the opinion that this review was written by Torrens; see Ricardo, *Letters . . . to . . . Trower*, p. 170, and Ricardo, *Letters . . . to McCulloch*, p. 52. Viner is of the opinion that this review was written by McCulloch.

[52] Compare the way in which he jumped in his population theory from political economy to metaphysical biology.

therefore mean the concrete accumulation of capital, this investment must always equal savings.

A STABLE MONETARY STANDARD   The first phase of the development of a monetary standard [53] was characterized by gradual regularization of the trade relations between early industrial England and other countries on the one hand, and the integration of the industrial mode of production within England on the other. The trade relations with foreign countries were characterized by an importation of raw materials and luxury goods and an exportation of finished industrial goods. Negatively, we may say that this period was most significant, as far as our problem here is concerned, because the export of capital, that is, the process of making the world uniform and integrating it through the industrial mode of production, had not yet begun to play any significant role.

The result of this state of affairs for what was meant by and what actually was the function of a "monetary standard" was that such a standard played a very concrete role as a physical measure for the values to be exchanged. Only gradually, and even then only as far as England as an economic unit was concerned, did the concept "monetary standard" begin to include the notion of accumulation.

This change in the basic position from which the monetary standard was being viewed implied much more than we have as yet indicated. Mercantilism had been the period of transition toward the concept of the economic individual. Through it the feudal notion that the individual was part of a larger organism, that man existed in God, and that the laws governing the behavior of man were indestructible and unchangeable laws, set by the whole of the organism and that meant God, had changed into its very opposite, namely, that the behavior of man was a direct manifestation of the existing divinity and a "good" life could be achieved only by being individually in as economically successful a manner as possible.[54]

[53] See Chapter III, above.

[54] Tawney, *Religion and the Rise of Capitalism;* also Weber, *The Protestant Ethic and the Spirit of Capitalism.*

This seems to be far from the narrow point under discussion. The attitude expressed in the theoretical understanding of the function of a monetary standard cannot be understood properly, however, without some clarity concerning the general outlook upon their contemporary world of the men who conceived it. And we should like to emphasize that this reference to the general social development as expressed in changing philosophies is not to be thought of as a mere historical reference, that is, as the introduction of a factor extraneous to the problem at hand. We conceive of all social, philosophical, ethical, psychological, and so forth, as well as economic, phenomena as manifestations of an interdependent social structure. We have indicated the socio-economic structural changes responsible for the change in the general outlook which was increasingly evident in the decades around the turn of the eighteenth century.

The changed concept of the individual is to be understood as a direct reflection of the growth of the industrial entrepreneur in the Adam Smith sense of this term. The very fact that economic activity was increasingly thought of as the resultant of a multitude of homogeneous individual actions, all exhibiting the same fundamental characteristics of self-interest, led necessarily to the formulation of superstructural concepts, that is, concepts which expressed the uniformity of action on the part of the economic individuals.

In the bullion controversy this process of formulating superstructural concepts is clearly exhibited. It is needless to say that similar processes could have been observed at that same time in other phases of social life. These, however, are not a part of the subject matter of this study. As far as the formulation of a theory of a monetary standard is concerned, the concepts employed began to exhibit during the course of the bullion controversy an interesting and highly important divergence from economic reality.

To make clear this divergence between theory and reality, we shall refer briefly to an historical phenomenon of a previous period with the warning that such an analogy can only

serve the purpose of illustrating a specific point and of bringing certain characteristics of this point into the foreground.
Analogies as such can never serve as an analytical tool.

The phenomenon we have in mind is the emergence of
public credit in the period of the High Renaissance. In that
period we can observe the necessity of delegating powers to
the "state" to provide for the formation of institutions in line
with and guaranteeing the newly developed trade. This created
the parallel need of financing the social integration of the
state. The basis did not yet exist on which an effective system
of taxation for the financing of this activity would be possible; as a matter of fact this was one of the goals to be achieved
in the process of forming national states. Until this period,
the only way to finance the state was by means of various types
of loans to the elected, or rather selected, sovereigns. This
sovereign, however, was mortal and so were his economic and
political functions. In order to insure the political continuity
of the nation, there occurred a rebirth, though in quite different form, of political heredity. Parallel with the political
continuity, emerged an abstract concept of debt, which insured the continuity of debt by making the life of the sovereign continuous, *in abstracto*. The interesting point to us in
this development is the fact that not only was the superstructural concept of "debt" formulated, but also this abstrac-
tion coexisted with, although as yet it influenced only slightly,
private individual monetary ownership.

If we return to the period of early industrial society, we
find that the preceding national integration of industrial production brought about a situation somewhat similar to that
described above.

With the appearance of production on a larger industrial
scale and the concomitant changes in the organizational and
financial aspects of this production, as manifested, for example, in the development of "anonymous" joint-stock companies, the impetus of economic activity passed from the
independent individual entrepreneur to the collaborative
productive entities. This development, as we have repeatedly

said, was accompanied by and as a matter of fact was a result of a higher integration of the national system of production. The integration was necessarily accompanied by the formulation of such superstructural concepts as "monetary standard," "the laws of supply and demand," "the theory of value," and others. Despite the change in the character of that economic individual from whose point of view after all the economic reality was seen, we find that the superstructural concepts continued to be imbued with the same characteristics with which the observing economic individuals had been accustomed to think of their own social and economic function at the time of the inception of the concepts. The gradually developing manager part-owners who had a tendency to become manager nonowners, as well as the correspondingly growing number of absentee owners, all conceived of themselves as being still the main actors in the process of production, as they undoubtedly had been during the preceding period which Adam Smith had described. The same error in the perception of contemporary reality and of their function in it was manifested in their perception of other functions within the given national economy. To understand, therefore, the theory of money of the late Ricardian period and the function which a monetary standard was supposed to play means to take into account this necessary margin of error in judgment. There arises, thus, in this period the attitude of thinking in terms of "economic systems" divorced for the first time in the period of industrial production from economic reality. The difference cannot be too greatly emphasized between the post-Ricardian systematizing and the attempts to understand economic actions integrally, that is, in terms of systems as employed from the late mercantilists up to Ricardo.

These introductory remarks were necessary for an understanding of the problem with which this section deals; namely, with the question of the stability of a monetary standard. It will now be clear from the preceding paragraphs that the term "stability" as used at that time is capable of a twofold interpretation from our point of view. We must distinguish between that function of stability which, according to our analysis of the productive process of that time, actually existed and was realizable and the notion of stability used by the economic theoreticians of the time and referred to in their respective "systems." The evaluation of the latter can be attempted only after the "margin of error," of which we spoke, has been determined.

The outstanding characteristic of the process of production during the period under consideration was, as far as the problem of a stable monetary standard was concerned, to safeguard the continuity of the created and existing interests in the different "factors" of production. As far as production in the narrower sense of the word was concerned, the outstanding interest was in its maintenance as a means of continuing profits on the invested capital. Being divorced from the actual process of production, either by means of absentee investment or its complementary opposite, lack of investment, this interest in the continuity of profit began to center around the maintenance of the originally invested capital. This idea, then, was pursued, irrespective of all those economic changes which to varying degrees and over varying periods were continuously rendering previous capital investments obsolete. This attitude was most strongly put forward by the investing groups, while the part-owning or non-owning managers, who were for obvious reasons amenable to this point of view, began to stress the particular problem with which they were directly concerned. This problem was, if the general task was to maintain investments, to prevent any danger to investments from becoming acute. Such a danger, from the partisan point of view of the producer, was the possibility of increasing costs, and this danger was emphasized by the numerical increasing of competitors in production. It is interesting to notice here that the consumers' point of view began to assert itself very slowly, and when it had asserted itself as the outlook of the absentee owners, we find that the latter encountered little difficulty in combining the pseudo-producer point of view with the more crude pleasure-pain principles of the English utilitarians into that subjective economic theory which, after the timid beginnings of J. B. Say and, later, of Hermann Gossen and Stanley Jevons, became known as the marginal utility school of economics.

The point to be made here in connection with the attitude of the managers of production is that their notion of stability was largely identified with stability in the cost of production. But this sort of interest in the stability of the price level was not the same as the price level stability with which modern economists were (and some still are) concerned, which is based essentially on the consuming absentee owner point of view.

Desire for stability in these terms was approximately realistic only under the conditions of an expanding national economy. By this we mean that while difficulties in disposing of the products of production were by no means entirely absent, they were relatively small and not generally and equally noticeable. This was the case in the period in which the increase in the productive apparatus and volume of output was accompanied by the transformation of the whole national population into industrial consumers.

The middleman, a type of merchant quite different from any of the previous agents, developed to serve the needs of the consumer group. He was increasingly interested in the maintenance of stable prices and was the first to give emphasis to the need for stability in the general price level, especially in a period in which the prices showed a tendency to fall. It is the explanation of this tendency of the prices to fall with which we have been concerned. How, then, do we see these and other points reflected in the contemporary theories?

If we attempt some kind of classification of the contemporary theoretical views cited previously, we do not mean to suggest that the personal histories of these writers explain the exact reasons for their preference for one approach or another. The danger of such crude and misunderstood individual sociology, when applied to scientific investigation, can find its counterpart only in the efforts made to explain economic phenomena with reference to "pure" and "received" doctrine. In general, we conceive of economic trends within given periods of society, these trends being manifestations of the productive relations existing at that given time. Without implying that each banker, manufacturer, or laborer, as an individual, must necessarily hold a specific point of view, it is possible, according to such a method of analysis, to determine the typical banker's, manufacturer's, trader's, or laborer's point of view.

Huskisson was a banker, and even when he became Chancellor of the Exchequer he felt and acted consciously or subconsciously as a trustee of the banker group, identifying naïvely, as is so customary, the interests of his group with those of society. To the economic interests of that group deflation was even more dangerous than inflation. Sinking prices meant not only sinking real values but also lessened ability to repay loans. It is therefore only natural to find Mr. Huskisson advocating a stable currency with moral as well as economic arguments. To him devaluation was "a stale and wretched expedient." [55]

Torrens, from a similar point of view, proposed practically that the currency could be kept stable if enough of a leeway were provided between the gold points in order to prohibit too early and easy an effect upon the currency at home of gold movements occasioned by the varying condition of the balance of payments. It is for this reason that he opposed the abolition of the laws prohibiting the export of coin and the melting of domestic coins and that later he advocated an increase in the customs duties. As Viner has pointed out, Torrens was willing to maintain the stability of the price level thus achieved, even if the process of achieving it "would involve a loss of the advantages of the 'territorial division of employment,' " as in Torrens's opinion a fall in the price

[55] Huskisson, *The Question Concerning the Depreciation of Our Currency Stated*, p. 18.

level was of sufficient harm to outweigh the possible profit from international trade.[56]

We have discussed earlier the ideas of Thomas Joplin on the question of the desirability of a stable price level. While Huskisson's and Torrens's views can with relative ease be classed as being occasioned by the desire to maintain the existing value of currency, the reasons for Joplin's views are more complex. Joplin was a pioneer of joint-stock banking and as such much more intimately connected with the manufacturers than were the London private bankers or the directors of the Bank of England. In effect, however, his arguments differ little from those mentioned above. His main interest was the stability of the price level at home, that is, in England and Ireland, and he was perfectly willing to make the export trade suffer by stopping gold payments if it were likely that conditions at home would be affected adversely by such gold exports and prices consequently lowered.

John Rooke's point of view was not that of a banker or an absentee owner. His object was to maintain a stable price level in order to insure stability of cost of production. He advocated increasing the volume of paper currency if prices should show a tendency to decline, and, writing in a period of deflation, it was easy for him to add to his proposal that this principle of varying the volume of paper should be applied also in the case of rising prices. This proposal reminds one of the reasoning of certain modern business-cycle theorists, who say that in times of depressions wages must be lowered and promise that in the next period of prosperity prices will not be allowed to rise again. But while wages are actually lowered, avoiding the next depression by preventing the prices from rising is usually forgotten or only rhetorically honored when prosperity actually arrives.

It was fortunate for Rooke's argument that prices did not rise. In order to provide a measure of value, he wished to

---

[56] *Cf.*, Viner, *Studies in the Theory of International Trade*, p. 207; also Torrens, *An Essay on Money and Paper Currency*, pp. 56 ff.

retain the precious metals as a constituent part of the currency exchangeable with the paper currency at any time, but instead of having the paper currency vary according to the fluctuations in the price of the precious metals, he wished to vary the precious-metal content of the standard of value according to the fluctuations in the price of the precious metals. Here we have an excellent example of the confusion produced by the above-mentioned newly developing method of rationalizing—in the form of theorizing. The fact which was so dear to the mercantilists and still cherished by Adam Smith and David Ricardo was entirely forgotten: that money was after all a means to an end, a medium in the operations of the process of production and distribution. As Ricardo said:

> It is . . . worthy of observation that so deep-rooted is the prejudice which considers coin and bullion as things essentially differing in all their operations from other commodities, that writers greatly enlightened upon the general truth of political economy seldom fail . . . to forget . . . and argue upon the subject of money, and the laws which regulate its export and import, as quite distinct and different from those which regulate the export and import of other commodities.[57]

What Ricardo maintains with reference to the export and import of money, we want to extend here to the process of production as a whole.

The increase in the division of labor in its intellectual reflection manifested the increasing inability of the theorists to look beyond their own and immediate special interests. Rooke was interested in the stability of the prices of production, and consequently he proposed to use as a measuring stick for the value of the currency the "annual price of farm labor," to be modified, because of the lag in the adjustment of farm wages to changes in prices of commodities and because of the natural fluctuations of harvests, by the wages in the export industries.[58] If fluctuations in the value of precious metals result

---

[57] Cf. Ricardo, *Works*, p. 292.
[58] Rooke, *An Inquiry into the Principles of National Wealth*, p. 88; also *Remarks on the Nature and Operation of Money*.

from the balance of payments between different countries, then a negative balance of payments must also be allowed to react upon the internal price level; otherwise the proposal to prevent it from acting upon the internal price level assumes the form of an opportunistic policy, which does not care about the long-run results, rather than of an adequate theoretical explanation.[59] In a somewhat similar manner, Henry James advocated stabilization of prices by using wheat and farm labor as measures of value.[60] While John Rooke still adhered to a convertible paper currency, Thomas Attwood was willing to go a great deal farther to achieve the same end. He advocated a government-regulated paper currency managed by means of open-market operations in national debt certificates.[61] As a standard of value, he proposed to use the price of wheat, which seemed at that time most representative of the general status of the price level and of the purpose for which the currency was to be managed. He realized, as Henry James did not, that the price for labor always tended to exhibit a lag as compared to the moment at which a change took place in the volume of currency, with an accompanying effect upon the prices. And since

five percent interest per annum, which has so long been established by law, and approved by universal custom and consent, seems now to have become a kind of par in the value of money, by the means of which we may at all times judge of the efficiency of the circulating medium,

[59] Irving Fisher has "acknowledged Rooke as an anticipator of his own 'compensated dollar' plan" (Viner, *Studies in the Theory of International Trade*, p. 208). It will be clear from our exposition that there can be no meaningful direct reference between the doctrine of Fisher and that of John Rooke for the reason that their respective theorizing was concerned with fundamentally different sets of economic data. On the other side, a similar, though by no means the same, argument as that used against Rooke can be advanced against Fisher. Fisher's compensated dollar as a device of economic policy can operate only as long as the influences from outside the national economy (but nevertheless belonging to the same general economic structure of which national industrial economies after all are only parts) have not as yet made themselves felt.

[60] James, *Essays on Money, Exchanges and Political Economy*.

[61] Attwood, *Prosperity Restored*, pp. 131 ff.; Attwood, *Observations on Currency, Population, and Pauperism*, pp. 166 ff.; and Attwood, *The Late Prosperity and the Present Adversity of the Country Explained*, pp. 34-35.

Attwood concluded that "the rate of interest is perhaps as good a criterion as the bushel of wheat." [62] In addition, however, Attwood proposed that "the par of labor . . . would, probably, be a more certain guide than the rate of interest, and would not be so obnoxious to popular prejudice as the bushel of wheat." [63] Attwood did not deceive himself into taking for granted a direct relation between the volume of currency to be issued and a demand for money. Such a direct relation would exist only under the condition of available "beneficial" employment, and full employment is the main criterion according to which a monetary policy had to be directed. "Whenever . . . the money of a country is sufficient to call every laborer into action, upon the system and trade best suited to his habits and his powers, the benefits of an increased circulation can go no further." [64]

The important difference between the various schools advocating a stable monetary standard can thus not be brought to light by making a distinction between the support of a convertible metallic and a nonconvertible paper standard of money, but by the different aspects of the main interest each had in wanting to change the existing state of monetary affairs and according to the purpose for which they wished to change the existing monetary techniques. The complaint that there was not sufficient explicit argument advanced by the advocates of a convertible metallic standard against those who were rather in favor of a nonconvertible paper standard therefore explains itself.[65] Having their practical purpose quite definitely, though not always explicitly, in mind, the advocates of the various proposals were willing to use any means to support their arguments as long as it suited their ends.

This position can be seen still more clearly in the proposals of those who argue in more pronounced extremes. The Earl of Rosse has perhaps put most clearly the attitude fundamentally held by most of the different schools, but not advanced

---

[62] Attwood, *Prosperity Restored*, p. 183.   [63] *Ibid.*, p. 184.
[64] Attwood, *A Letter to Nicholas Vansittart, on the Creation of Money, and on Its Action upon the National Prosperity*, p. 68.
[65] Viner, *Studies in the Theory of International Trade*, p. 214.

with equal clarity by all of them, because few could indulge in the luxury of such full detachment from actual and particular economic problems as his lordship was able to do. He was

inclined to think that the wants of man, and the ingenuity exercised in remedying them as they occurred, have in this, as in most other instances, formed, upon the whole, a better system of currency for this country at present, and better adapted to the circumstances of the time, than any statesman, or political economist, however able and well informed, could have devised in his closet . . . the thing is done first; the reason why it should be done is found out afterwards.[66]

This classic and extreme statement of a *laissez faire, laissez passer* attitude is represented, too, in the attitudes of those whose interest in easy money led them to look for justification for their demands wherever they could find it. Sir John Sinclair, for instance, pointed out that the considerable increase in commerce and public revenue demanded an increased volume of circulating medium, this necessary increase to be provided by new issues of bank notes. In connection with this demand Ricardo asked quite clearly, "Who has denied it?" [67] The only question important to Ricardo was: "How much money should circulate?" And to this problem Sir John Sinclair advanced no answer. In the crudest form, equaled only by later equilibrium theorists, he (Sinclair) considered money absolute and took it for granted that an increase of paper circulating would directly reduce the rate of interest. Assuming that

the total circulation of Great Britain . . . be 40 millions sterling in coin and in paper, bearing an interest of five per cent . . . [then] if it were reduced to 30 millions, bearing an interest of six per cent how much would not the industry of the nation be cramped? Whereas, were it raised to 50 millions, bearing an interest of four per cent and the whole of it actively employed in

[66] Rosse, *Observations on the Present State of the Currency of England*, pp. 87–88.

[67] Ricardo, "Letter to the *Morning Chronicle* on Sinclair's 'Observations,' " September 18, 1810, *Minor Papers on the Currency Question, 1809–1823*, ed. by J. H. Hollander, p. 73.

various industrious pursuits, it cannot be doubted, that the prosperity of the country would be increased with celerity, and carried to a height, which would not otherwise have been attainable.

Ricardo adds to this that "if this reasoning be just, how incalculable would the prosperity of the country become, if the bank would increase their notes to 100 millions and lend them at three per cent." [68] Sinclair identified money with the supply and demand for capital much as savings and investment are continually confused today.

The most basic issue in periods of deflation could not be and was never fully realized by any of the contemporary economists. The fact that economy was expanding was obvious and not denied. But to be able to interpret this expansion as a structural change in the national economy, it would have been necessary to observe not only the effects of an expanding economy but also the changes resulting from an economy which began gradually to contract. The latter, however, became only gradually noticeable in the last half of the nineteenth century and, for that matter, are not even fully accepted by economic theorists today. For this reason it is only natural that the deflation phase was interpreted in general as a temporary effect of particular economic-political actions and that the removal of the causes for such effects would do away entirely with the observed and deplored consequences. We have tried to show that most of the explanations for the deflation were founded in historical fact, but that these historical facts did not represent all the causes or, which is even more important, the most basic causes.

For the sake of simplicity, we will give major emphasis to the decreasing cost of production, as manifested by the changing economic structure, with the implied aspects of intensely increasing competition, increasing investment and fixed capital, and the growing contradiction between the desired continuity in the value of investments, on the one hand, and decreasing prices and the increased rate of obsolescence, on the other. This gives some indication of the economic reality

[68] *Ibid.*, p. 76.

within which the "stability" of the monetary standard was to be established. Another reason why the impossibility of establishing a stable (and that meant static within the framework of the prevailing theory) monetary standard was not recognized is to be found in the fact that several tendencies of this same economic reality acted to obscure the previously mentioned ones. While competition was increasing in intensity, while average profits seemed to decrease, and while the relation between fixed and variable capital was changing in favor of the former, the absolute volume of production, as well as the number of potential consumers, was still increasing. This produced the illusion that profits were not seriously endangered and as far as the total volume was concerned seemed to be rather increasing than otherwise. The cause for the declining price level, then, was said to be monetary measures, and the structural changes responsible for this decline were barely mentioned.

A second cause for the existing failure adequately to perceive the function of money at that time is that the industrial system of production, with the mechanism of which we are here concerned, had not yet become fully operative outside England, except in some rather isolated spots on the Continent. The working of the exchange rates by the different countries was therefore still based to a considerable, though of course changing, extent upon trade-capitalist relations, at least in so far as most of the foreign countries were concerned with mercantile trade or manufactural production rather than with industrial production as it had become distinct and predominant in England.

However, this does not imply that, even though industrial, the forces then operating in England in foreign trade were of the same kind as those that operated in the last half of the nineteenth century, to say nothing of the economic forces in foreign trade today. One of the important manifestations of an industrial society that is progressing and expanding beyond national boundaries was still insignificant, if not functionally, at least absent, that is, the export of capital.

In the following chapter we shall discuss some of these problems in their direct relation to the function of money. At this moment we wish only to point out that the much-complained-of lack of interest in the foreign-exchange aspects of the theory of money was not accidental at all. The reality which later gave rise to the discussions about its intricate and changing nature simply did not exist at that time.

During the period of the bullion controversy the role of the exchange rates as far as they affected the stability of the monetary standard was considered in the main as that of an extraneous force, the operation of which was important only when it affected the national currency adversely. Quite correctly, it was perceived that the emphasis for the determination of the most beneficial monetary policy had to be laid upon the functioning of the monetary standard at home, that it was more important to have "a steady currency and fluctuating exchanges" than "steady exchanges and a fluctuating currency." [69] It was also thought to be more important to protect the home market from further causes for declining prices, thus giving the manufacturers a chance for increased exports, than to protect the consumer from rising prices.

With little export of capital and only isolated competition in production from abroad, the basis for the working of the exchange rates as later perceived by Mill was not yet fully developed. Consequently, there was no reason for preferring a metallic standard on the assumption that it facilitated or stabilized international trade. On this basis it would have been impossible for any economist at that time to set forth theoretical explanations of the relations "between stable and unstable exchanges, and between a metallic standard and a paper standard" or to recognize that "the important issue," supposedly, was "only as and if the former in operation provides stable exchanges and the latter in operation fails to do so." Fluctuations of the exchanges are part and parcel of

[69] Bollmann, *A Second Letter . . . on the Practicability of the New System of Bullion Payments,* p. 25n; see also Walter Hall, *A View of Our Late and of Our Future Currency,* p. 56; George Woods, *Observations on the Present Price of Bullion,* p. 53.

that system of production which produced the commodities in foreign trade, and "foreign investment" can be affected by fluctuating exchanges only in so far as such investment already exists.

SOME TENTATIVE CONCLUSIONS ON THE THEORY OF DEFLATION
The position taken here regarding the general and structural forces underlying the formulation of the classical theory of deflation may be summarized briefly in the following way: The general character of the rise in the general price level is due to the fact that the changes in the process of production, particularly those in the institutions concerned with the supply of fixed and circulating capital, made for a marked decrease in the scarcity of this supply. Competition resulted in higher accumulation and a tendency toward lower prices. This tendency was enforced by the still lagging supply of labor. Also, the agricultural revolution contributed gradually to a decrease in the price of the mobile factor of production.

A supposed contraction of currency, as previously advocated to counteract inflationary tendencies, was, however, blamed for injury to industry resulting from the fall of prices. By using the reasoning employed to explain inflation, deflation was thought to represent the simple opposite of inflation. The industrial producer was thought to suffer from forced savings caused by a supposed oversupply of commodities. The conclusion, by inference, was that voluntary savings should equal investment and that this relation between savings and investment was to be kept equal by a flexible rate of interest. The demand for relative stability in the relation between volume and value of money was thus a mere rationalization and a pious hope for counteracting the increasingly intense competition with its resultant decline in prices and relative rigidity in the minimum price of labor.

The deflationary phase of early industrial society did not produce the complete formulation of a theory of money. While the general outline of such a theory became gradually visible because of the completion of the national economic integration in England, the elimination of the mercantile frontiers and the transformation of this outside world into industrial countries, with the consequent quasi-automatic working of the international exchange rates, was necessary to make possible the final formulation of the classical quantity theory of money. Combined with the previously developed theory of inflation, the theory of deflation as developed after the resumption of cash payments was to form the complementary part in an equilibristic theory of money.

9 · The Quantity Theory of Money

What she reveals not to thy mental sight
Thou wilt not wrest from her with curves and calculations.
                                                    GOETHE.

I N an analysis of the transmutations of the function of
money and the accompanying changes in the doctrines
dealing with these changes one can observe that up to the
time of the Currency Debates no fully developed and self-
supporting "theory of money" had yet been formulated. With
the growing domination of the industrial mode of production
over the whole of English social life, the scope of the social
and economic phenomena affected and permeated by money
—the symbolic manifestation of the industrial exchange economy—broadened considerably. Contrary to the a-national
character of the economic concepts of the preceding period,
the type of analysis of the economic organism of society developing in the early nineteenth century, for example, in the
Ricardian interpretation, was presented on a national basis,
that is, the "principles of national economy" were investigated, not the later abstract neoclassical "principles of economics."

THE CHANGED FUNCTION OF INTERNATIONAL TRADE Industrial
production, however, did not remain, nor in the strictest
sense of the term was it ever, a national phenomenon. Exports of industrially produced goods played a role from the
very beginning of this type of production. Up to the early
decades of the nineteenth century the importance of these
exports was overshadowed by the ability of the English producers, the pioneers of industrial society, to dispose of their
output in the national market, which increased with the growing industrialization of the country and with the accompanying transformation of a growing number of the people into
active participants in this industrial production and therewith into consumers of the products produced. In reaching
the stage of relative national industrial integration, that is,

having transformed England into a predominantly industrial country, the need for new effective outlets for the increasing output of the country assumed added importance. It is not suggested here that the consumptive propensity of England became exhausted. Quite the contrary was the case. Every increase in consuming power from that time on, however, appeared necessarily as an increase in cost of production. This danger, in turn, was met by the growth of inventions and the consequent application of labor-saving devices. The effectiveness of this attempt to halt the decline of average profits was limited by the increased intensity of competition and the changing form of enterprise as small-scale private production became replaced in relative importance by large-scale corporate enterprise. Under these conditions it became mandatory not only to find new outlets for the produced commodities but also to find a new way to decrease costs. It was due to this need to decrease costs, in a period of falling prices, that the possibility of utilizing cheaper labor, that is, labor in not yet industrially developed countries, was discovered.

This type of expansion of industrial society, that is, the extension of the English industrial type of producing commodities beyond the original national boundaries, is covered by the term "capital export."[1] Capital export was the solution to both of the main problems of English production. It provided a tremendous impulse to English commodity export in the form of capital goods exports. The capital invested in these machines was put to work with less labor cost than would have been possible at home, and at the same time it created new and growing markets for finished consumer goods by transforming the foreign laborers into industrial consumers. This state of affairs is fundamentally different from the earlier, mercantile, type of foreign trade at a time when the relation of England to other countries, whether overtly or only indirectly "colonial," consisted in the exchange of finished goods for raw materials or finished goods for luxury goods.

[1] Niebyl, "Historijske Izmjene u Funkciji Izvoza Kapitala," *Ekonomist* (Zagreb), V (July–August, 1939), 284 ff.

After the advent of capital export international trade increasingly assumed that form which had previously prevailed in the national scene.

It is this change in the character of foreign trade, its becoming an inherent part of industrial production, that completes the formation of an international industrial economy. The theory of foreign trade as it was now expressed by John Stuart Mill, rounded out the classical theory of economic mechanics and produced with it, as we shall see, the classical theory of money.

THE CURRENCY DEBATES   It will now be our task to follow in some detail the steps which led to the final formulation of the classical theory of money. The point of discussing in this connection the famous "Currency Debates" is not merely to communicate historical events and therefore to adhere in the presentation to the overt forms in which the Debates were clothed. The problem here is to discover that economic process of which the Debates were the doctrinal products.

The particular content of the Currency Debates provides direct evidence that the general problems of industrial production in its ascending phase had, for that phase, been solved. For example, in the Debates much emphasis was placed upon the problem of the operation of international exchange. This problem, however, was not treated as an issue of general economic analysis. The latter was taken for granted, and the Debates were focused upon what has been called in the literature on this subject a "short-run issue." The reason for such concentration on short-run issues is not appreciated by some economists.[2] The issue about which the Currency Debates arose was on the surface the same one which we treated in our last paragraph on the bullion controversy: to determine the standard which would best serve the English economy. More concretely, these Debates were concerned with that one point

[2] Gregory, *Select Statutes Documents and Reports Relating to British Banking 1832–1928*, I, ix; also Viner, *Studies in the Theory of International Trade*, p. 218.

which the contemporary theorists felt was very inadequately treated, namely, the mechanism operative in the relation between England and other countries.

The difficulty encountered here by the interpreting economists is highly interesting. This transition from the discussion and analysis of general principles or long-run issues to the very possibility of engaging in the analysis of particular events or short-run issues is important in the process of thought formation regarding the nature and significance of the flow of money. This analysis considers some resulting implications in the present-day use of monetary concepts.

Before the significance of this problem is investigated, a slight deviation may be permissible. The difficulty in every historical and analytical presentation today is language.[3] The same frame of mind which, as we are trying to show, produced the quantitative notions of monetary theory and the static logic of nineteenth-century science tempts writers and readers to oversimplify historical processes by classifying them into more or less rigid phases which, however, do not exist in that inflexible form. If, therefore, we are maintaining that the period of the Currency Debates was characterized by a kind of foreign trade structurally different from that of the Bullion Controversy, we do not mean to say that the basic elements of the former were not already present in the latter. What we do want to say is that only after 1830 had they developed to such an extent that they gradually achieved major importance. Consequently, aside from the effects resulting from foreign wars, the movements of precious metals were determined in the period preceding the Currency Debates largely by the state of production at home and the possibility of disposing of products, or of buying the commodities to be imported, in accordance with the status of the national economy. The flow thus determined was only modified by the state of the supply of precious metals abroad. After the 1830's, however, when the national economy was actively engaged in ex-

---

[3] Fraser, *Economic Thought and Language;* also Niebyl, "The Need for a Concept of Value in Economic Theory," *Quarterly Journal of Economics,* February, 1940, pp. 201 ff.

tending its economic boundaries, the rules according to which precious metals began to move to and from England were set by conditions of production on both sides of the English frontier. If we add to this the fact that the first formative stage of industrial society had been passed and the interrelations within this new society had become well regularized, we will understand that the mechanism exhibited in the movement of the foreign exchanges began to show the same characteristics of apparent automatism that were observed in the preceding period in the relation of the London metropolis to the provinces.[4]

How, then, did contemporary economists think that foreign exchanges operated? On the one side it was maintained that any efflux of gold to or influx from foreign countries must produce an automatic and corresponding decrease or increase in the volume of money in circulation. The Currency School maintained that inasmuch as automatic operation was obvious in the case of a metallic currency, a paper currency based on a metallic standard should be made to operate in the same way. It was fully recognized that a paper currency would not necessarily operate automatically in the same way that metallic currency operated, and it was therefore advocated that certain rules for monetary management should be laid down. If such rules were not established and followed there would be danger in the possibility of issuing paper money in excess of, or of contracting it at other times in undue proportion to, the needs of the national economy.

The obvious inference in this type of argument is that prices should be made to vary according to the needs of international trade. We have to remember that foreign trade no longer remained the exclusive domain of the London merchants, but, because of its change in character, was now of equal, if not greater, importance to the country manufacturer. It is important to keep this direction of the argument of the

[4] The newly developing contradictory tendencies of the productive organism are here consciously neglected, since we are going to stop with our analysis at a point at which their importance had not yet become predominant.

so-called Currency School in mind because it will be found that it is similar to that of the Banking School and that both differ only in regard to the techniques by which the smooth operation of the monetary standard, and that meant smooth monetary relations between England and foreign countries, was to be achieved. The members of the Currency School were more realistic in their formulation and analysis of the problem and more traditional at the same time. While they were willing to grant the automatic working of the price mechanism over the long run, they were induced by the experience of the preceding period of inflation into being cautious about giving entirely free way to the principles of absolute *laissez faire* as advocated by the Banking School. The Banking School, represented by men like John Fullerton, Thomas Tooke, J. W. Gilbert, and others, played the role of His Majesty's loyal opposition by laying emphasis on the general principles, on the one hand, and on the other hand by directing its critique against any of the practical proposals made by the other side. To the Banking School governmental or any regular control exerted upon the flow of money seemed anathema. According to this School the only effective control operated automatically within the economy of that time—by means of the all-leveling competition. If bankers were willing to issue notes in excess of what could safely be absorbed by business, and if business were willing to take credits in excess of its needs, both would have to pay the inevitable penalty of inflation.

The particular arguments advanced for and against each one of the techniques consisted mainly in attempts to clarify the workings and the mechanics of the flow of money in particular cases. Thus, it was pointed out that the velocity of paper notes was not the same as that of metallic coins and that, therefore, any increase or decrease in the volume of precious metals would have to be accompanied by a larger decrease or increase in the volume of notes outstanding in order to attain the correct proportion between the increase or decrease in the volume of notes and coins. As this greater velocity of notes, as compared to that of coins, could be shown to exist, but could not be measured accurately, any attempt to regulate the volume of notes in circulation in accordance with the volume of coins was said to be arbitrary. The Banking School also pointed out that the volume of money in circulation may not consist exclusively of currency, but that an increasing part may be represented by deposits. In the latter case any control of the volume of money had to include control over the deposits in order to be at all effective. In addition, the point was made, though with much less justification, that gold would not necessarily move from and to the country in direct proportion to the status of the trade balance. This, the Banking School held, might be due to the hoarding of gold, and any fluctuation in the nation's currency might be the result of an increase or decrease of these hoards rather than the international movement of gold.[5] The Banking School, however, never made clear why such hoards should have existed. It could not have been argued that they were due to the existence or nonexistence of confidence, as Malthus incorrectly argued, because it was lack of confidence which was to be avoided by the smooth operation of a monetary standard. Hoarding was a point appropriately taken up by theorists in mercantile times when there were still large areas in the economic structure in which nonmanufacturing groups were in existence. In an integrated industrial economy there is no room for hoards except in two cases. First, for reasons of temporary lack of confidence, and such lack of confidence would have to be a product of the working of that system itself and therefore could not really be considered one of the conditions; secondly, if the economy as a whole should come to an impasse in which investment possibilities were permanently below the available supply of funds.

The sanctioning of a number of new monetary techniques gave added evidence of the progressing change in the econ-

[5] Fullerton, *On the Regulation of Currency*, p. 140.

omy. Several legislative enactments had established for England practically a pure gold standard. The operation of the
latter was greatly strengthened in 1826 when finally all notes
below £5 were taken out of circulation. The Act of 1833 not
only made the Bank of England notes legal tender but also
removed the restriction of a maximum interest rate of 5 percent on discounts of the Bank running for more than ninety
days. The banking facilities in the metropolis were greatly
broadened and improved by the permission to establish non-
note-issuing joint-stock banks within a 65-mile radius of London and the establishment of banks with more than six partners outside this same radius.

After most of the necessary technical and institutional
foundations for an automatically working monetary standard
had thus been prepared, the "Palmer rule" was established in
1827 by the Bank of England. This was the first practical
application of the currency principle to English banking
operations. This rule attempted to enforce the presumably
necessary identity between convertible paper currency and
metallic currency in its operation with respect to the exchange rates. Under its provisions the Bank of England attempted to keep a bullion reserve covering one-third of its
effective money circulation, that is, notes and deposits together. The remaining two-thirds was to be kept in securities,
the volume of these securities to remain constant in order to
insure that any increase or decrease in the amount of bullion
in the vaults of the Bank would react automatically upon the
volume of the means of exchange.[6]

No provision was made in this rule for determining the
strategy to be used with regard to deposits in case of gold
movements. The position of Pennington on this point is of
interest. In deviating from the rigid currency principle, he
maintained that notes as well as deposits should fluctuate with

[6] Palmer, *Evidence in the Report from the Commons Committee of Secrecy
on the Bank of England Charter*, p. 11; also Pennington, *A Letter to Kirkman Finlay, Esq., On the Importation of Foreign Coin and the Value of
Precious Metals in Different Countries*.

the gold movements.[7] At the same time, he did not believe that the existing deposits in the Bank of England could function as a cause of danger to the bullion reserve in times of stress by having these deposits withdrawn from the Bank in the form of bullion because "a larger portion of those deposits consists of the reserves of the private banks, which they are obliged to keep in hand, and which in times of pressure and alarm they find it expedient to increase rather than diminish."

Facts indicate, however, that for the period in question the volume of securities in the Bank showed a tendency to remain constant, the volume of the reserve varying considerably more than the volume of notes in circulation.[8]

There can be no doubt that this state of monetary affairs favored stability of the price level within the country at the expense of an increasing discrepancy between the English price level and that of the outside world. The result was that the hectic nature of the development of English industry at this period of productive expansion and falling prices was made worse by the instability of prices in the much-needed foreign trade, increasing thus the tendency toward crises by adding monetary hazards to the already existing and increasingly apparent cyclical nature of industrial production.

The advocates of the currency principle were well aware of the problems thus created, and Torrens, as well as Jones, emphasized that the Bank should hesitate to vary consciously the total volume of securities held by it if it were found that its reserve was being diminished by the withdrawal of deposits, since the stability in the relation of the reserves held to the amount of money circulating was their main objective.

[7] Pennington, *A Letter to Kirkman Finlay, Esq.*, pp. 89–90.

[8] "Taking average quarterly figures between 1832 and 1840, 'in that period the difference between the highest and lowest amount of deposits was £12,384,000; securities £10,804,000; bullion £8,178,000; whilst the difference between the highest and lowest amount of circulation, which ought to have varied with the influx or efflux of bullion, varied only to the extent of rather more than £3,000,000. The result of the action of the Bank was to keep their circulation even and to let their deposits, securities, and bullion vary.' " *House of Commons Debates*, Vol. LXXIV (series 3), 20th May, 1844, col. 1361, cited by Gregory, *Select Statutes*, I, p. xviii.

Constancy in the volume of security holdings was a means to be used only in times when it operated satisfactorily.[9] More particularly Jones and Torrens maintained that only the amount of the securities which served as the two-thirds of the necessary coverage for the note circulation should be kept constant, while the remainder should be made to vary according to the needs resulting either from the volume of loans outstanding or from the state of the currency. It is on this point that the advocates of the Currency Principle made one of their important proposals, one which was to have significance far beyond expectations at the time when it was made. They proposed to separate the banking department of the Bank of England from the issuing department in order to guarantee that the securities used to cover the notes issued would be kept separate from those held by the Bank as coverage for loans granted, the amount of which appeared in the books of the Bank in the form of deposits. It is obvious that such a proposal was based upon a conception of the role of the Bank of England as the central bank of the country, capable of regulating directly the total volume of notes being circulated in the country. As Viner has pointed out, the Currency School advocates did not emphasize this quiet assumption "as a precaution, perhaps, against providing further stimulus to the already vigorous opposition of the country bankers to the Currency School proposals." [10]

This separation of the banking and issuing departments was realized in the famous Peel's Act of 1844, commonly called the "Charter of English Banking." There is no need to go minutely into the subsequent operations under this Act. It will suffice to say here that while the Bank of England used the banking department as an instrument of attack upon the country banks to establish its predominance, by increasing the discounts at a rate of interest very low for that time, the sub-

[9] Overstone, *Tracts and Other Publications on Metallic and Other Paper Currency*, ed. by J. R. McCulloch, p. 29; see also Torrens, *A Letter to Lord Melbourne on the Considerations of the Recent Derangement in the Money Market*, p. 29.

[10] Viner, *Studies in the Theory of International Trade*, p. 229.

sequent crises were met by a suspension of the coverage provision for the issue of notes, which in every case proved to
alleviate satisfactorily the temporary panics. The reasons for
such positive operation, for example, in the crises of 1847,
1858, and 1866, are not, however, to be found exclusively in
the financial structure of the country, but rather in the process
of production. It was the overcoming of the productive rigidities of relatively small enterprises producing for national
trade, by the gradually-increasing utilization of new inventions and cheaper labor, aided by the extension of credit by
the central bank, which successfully resulted in unfreezing
otherwise sound debts and easing the necessary period of
transformation through bankruptcies and reorganizations.

In this process we find realized the principles advocated by
the Banking School. We find that the actual operation of the
English banking system, though not according to the letter
of the enacted laws or the adopted rules, was increasingly
successful in linking the operation of the foreign exchanges
with the financial mechanism of the country. We find also
that the reasoning on the "short-run issues" discussed logically
presupposed the tendency of the economy toward equilibrium. The mechanics of this continuing, though so far still
not continuous, harmony were more and more thought to be
set in motion by monetary causes, with the result that the
theorizing contemporary economists conceived the idea of
expressing the major economic laws in monetary terms.

THE THEORY OF EQUILIBRIUM   The middle of the nineteenth
century brought the completion of the process which transformed England and was transforming other countries into
fully developed units of industrial production. It also brought
an institutional change which, in addition to those previously
mentioned, enabled the industrial English economy to em-
bark upon that period of industrial progress which through
the absence of any major upheavals gave the appearance of a
now "mature" economy in equilibrium, within which the
minor disturbances assumed the character of temporary de-

viations. The repeal of the Corn Laws made it possible for the English producer to lower temporarily, though very effectively, the cost of production by decreasing wage costs without being forced to decrease any further the real wage. The overpowering difficulties created earlier by deflation and before that by inflation, receded into the background of economic consciousness, and while they were not forgotten, they were incorporated into a larger conception of the economic "laws," in which they appeared as temporary "deviations" of an otherwise "normal" trend.

Production and capital accumulation had thus found an effective means to continued growth. On the one hand, cheap labor was made available in relative abundance abroad, waiting only for the investment of the funds "saved" in England and transferred abroad through an increasingly active balance of trade. On the other hand, industry at home was temporarily relieved of the threat of a relative increase in cost because of the decreased cost of living of the laborers.

Under such conditions there was no conceivable reason for the expression of pessimism on the part of the English producers and industrial traders, the more so as this rise in profits allowed them to "appease" the social dissatisfaction for the time being. The Victorian middle classes were happily incapable of perceiving the dangers in their situation. They were encouraged in their temporarily warranted optimism by their equally temporary ability to pay for their peace of mind. The ability to rationalize which had developed at that time created a "political" disposition which was responsive to, if not responsible for, the idea of "static economic production," or a production moving in "equilibrium" with only temporary deviations which, once created by what were assumed to be "external" causes, must of mathematical necessity reestablish that very equilibrium by moving with the same intensity to the other side of the line of harmony.

The final formulation of a theory of economic equilibrium, particularly a monetary theory based on equilibrium concepts, is now, and only now, possible. In the manufacturing period, that is, the last stage of mercantilism and the first stage of industrial production, the notions concerning manufacture were crude and made to order for the solution of the particular problems at hand. In the first phase of industrial production these notions broadened, but they still corresponded largely to the economic reality which they were intended to express. With the gradual integration of industrial production, thinking in terms of an abstract and assumedly generally valid system began to prevail, and the theorists during that period began to treat their specific subjects of investigation always with reference to these a priori accepted general laws of industrial society.[11] While this logical, or at least methodological, system was in process of formulation, industrial production not only proceeded to permeate other countries but also began, in this process, to show important signs of difficulties attendant upon the resumption of full employment after prosperity had again been achieved. Average profits began to show, at least temporarily, menacing signs of a tendency to decrease, and the repeated difficulties in finding investments for savings again occasionally disquieted the manufacturing groups. The significance of the development of this type of theory lies in the fact that a veil was thrown over the actual thoroughgoing transmutation of the home economy. This discrepancy between the economic reality of that time as we understand it today and the form in which this reality appeared to contemporary economists was necessarily reflected in the economic thought of that time. The lag between systematic thought and economic reality remained unrecognized, to the extent that the temporary recuperation of

[11] It is not maintained here that those interested in economic problems in the later period of mercantilism did not attempt their solutions with reference to certain systems of philosophies. The outstanding difference between the mercantilist thinkers, and, for example, Adam Smith or Ricardo, consists in the fact that the former (and, analogically, the post-John Stuart Mill economists) referred to a system of thought created by and belonging to a period preceding the one within which the concrete problems with which they were dealing had sprung up. In consequence, these "systems" had to be abstract by nature and, therefore, were referring to "natural laws" and divine providence rather than to economic laws in the Ricardian sense.

profits enabled the entrepreneurs to recover for the time being.

Only on this basis, which excluded by its very nature the ability to recognize fundamental structural, that is, qualitative changes, was it possible to erect the magnificent building of a logically consistent, harmonious, and most definitely "closed" system of economic equilibrium theory. It was quite appropriate that at this time the term "political economy" was coming into disrepute. The term suggested that the method referred to would enable the people who used it to *direct consciously* their economic actions. But already Jean Baptiste Say recognized quite clearly that the "science" of political economy or, as it was later and perhaps more adequately called, "economic theory," was quite incapable, from then on, of being put to any such practical use. This judgment concerning the function of economic thinking was the result of a very real experience—namely, the inapplicability of contemporary economic thought to economic reality.

Ricardo, McCulloch, James Mill, and Nassau Senior considered all the important aspects of the process of production as aspects of some of the "great" economic laws. John Stuart Mill, in that greater part of his economic theory in which he was still predominantly a classicist, had for the last time summarized all the important findings of the old classical school. At the same time we can begin to see in him most clearly a new attitude arising, which will be the subject of our discussion elsewhere.

The best presentation, perhaps, of this development can be found in the concept and methodological tool of the *homo oeconomicus*. In it the subject matter treated by economic theory had lost the last semblance of economic reality, and it was not recovered for another thirty or forty years. Demand and supply, the relation of value and price, the laws of wages, profit, and rent, had finally found a summary crystallization in a theory of distribution based on Adam Smith's notions of production.[12] The working of the exchange rates with which

---

[12] In contradistinction to the theory of distribution by and after Stanley Jevons, H. Gossen, and E. v. Böhm-Bawerk.

the Currency Debates had been so painfully concerned no longer offered any problem. John Stuart Mill presents it very clearly.

> Disturbances . . . of the equilibrium of imports and exports, and consequent disturbances of exchange, may be considered as of two classes; the one occasional or accidental, if not on too large a scale, correct themselves through the premium on bills, without any transmission of the precious metals; the other arising from the general state of prices, which cannot be corrected without the subtraction of actual money from one of the countries, or an annihilation of credit equivalent to it; since the mere transmission of bullion (as distinguished from money), not having any effect on prices, is of no avail to abate the cause from which the disturbances proceed.[13]

And, logically conclusive, Mill continues that these "exchanges do not depend on the balance of debts and credits with each country separately, but with all countries taken together." [14] The *homo oeconomicus,* endowed with the character of unlimitable competitiveness, had achieved the right to move in the whole world. As this excludes by definition all other influences, even biological, though perhaps not geophysical, there was thus established a closed system, the harmony of which seemed insured and guaranteed.

THE CONCEPT QUANTITY   In describing the economic reality for the analysis of which he developed the use of mathematical tools, Cournot said that it developed from the most simple stage, characterized by "instinctive actions" to the complicated contemporary system in which "the abstract idea of *value in exchange* . . . supposes that the objects to which such value is attributed *are in commercial circulation; i.e.,* that it is always possible to find means to exchange them for other objects of equal value." [15] This development, in Cournot's opinion, was by no means at an end.

The extension of commerce and the development of commercial facilities tend to bring the actual condition of affairs nearer and

---

[13] Mill, *Principles of Political Economy,* p. 618.   [14] *Ibid.*
[15] Cournot, *Researches into the Mathematical Principles of the Theory of Wealth,* p. 8.

nearer to this order of abstract conceptions, *on which alone the-oretical calculations can be based* [italics ours], in the same way as the skillful engineer approaches nearer to theoretical conditions by diminishing friction through polished bearings and accurate gearing.[16]

It is important to realize the implications contained in this particular way of looking upon economic reality if we are to understand the meaning of the method applied at that time to analyze this reality. To repeat, the temporary overcoming of the main obstacles in the way of a continuation of a produc-tive, and with it consumptive, expansion permitted the con-ception of the process of production as being in balance, and the interpretation of the occurring and observed expansion as a mere extension in scope without any changes in the nature of the productive system itself. Of course, Cournot did not deny, nor did any of his contemporaries deny, the existence of frictions, but he thought of them in mechanical terms. Such analogies to mechanical devices were meaningful at the time in which they were made, because not only did the in-creasing mechanization of the process of production provide society with a major problem but also society itself, as we have just said, began to exhibit overtly the characteristics of a smoothly running machine. In the same way in which no difference was seen between the principle of a 10-horsepower steam engine and that of a 100-horsepower steam engine, the frictions in both cases were felt to be of a temporary kind, which perhaps made the machine vibrate, but were incapable of changing its character.

While Cournot thought of his contemporary economic so-ciety in typical nineteenth-century fashion as being "in har-mony," he inferred a causal development which led from the most simple stages of society up to the complicated contempo-rary society. In the latter "the influence of progressive civiliza-tion constantly tends to bring actual and variable relations nearer and nearer to the absolute relation which we attain to from abstract considerations."

[16] *Ibid.,* p. 9.

This, then, is another manifestation of the very basis upon which a mechanistic theoretical approach was possible. Only recently resurrected are the names of all the men who in their dealings with economic problems used mathematical tools.[17] These attempts to use algebraic formulations for the purpose of expressing varying relationships of economic data are part and parcel of and absolutely inseparable from the general method with the help of which economic problems, and as a matter of fact increasingly all problems, were viewed at that time. The development of this point of view has been presented above. It remains only to be said that such tools as algebraic equations cannot be separated from the general theory in which these tools function any more than pure theory can be divorced from the economic reality with which it had been created to deal.[18]

The ability to conceive of motion within a given system as a mere extension of that system has important implications as to the nature of the parts—the famous economic "data" of which the system was thought to exist. If progress could be conceived of as taking place in the form of a mere increase in quantity, the essential and fundamental laws of the system in motion would not have to be changed. Any one of the parts of the system was thus capable of being described in exclusively "quantitative" terms, the "quality" being related to the system as a whole and, under the stated conditions, static.

It would be beyond the scope of this inquiry to show, as can be shown conclusively, that Newtonian and as a matter of fact Euclidean terms, that is, static terms, are capable of

---

[17] See Marget, *The Theory of Prices*, pp. 10 ff. Mr. Marget recounts that "at least three algebraic formulations of the 'equation of exchange' in essentially the 'Fischerine' form were presented in the 1850's, namely, those of Roscher (1854), Bowen (1856), and Levasseur (1858)." See also *Journal of Political Economy*, XXXIII (1931), 574. Mr. Marget also calls attention "to the fact that K. H. Rau presented a Fischerine equation in 1841, *i.e.*, some thirteen years before Roscher. (See Rau, *Lehrbuch der politischen Ökonomie*, I, 305). But even before this time, Mr. Marget mentions, Henry Lloyd and his contemporary Italian economists used a crude formulation of an algebraic quantity equation "containing no term for 'velocity of circulation.'"

[18] For a directly opposite point of view see Marget, *The Theory of Prices*, Chapter II, especially p. 23.

dynamic interpretation. Riemann, for instance, demonstrated eighty years ago that the interpretation of Euclidean geometry prevailing at that time could be looked upon as a special case among a number of possible other cases.[19] To this we can add that the particular "case" of geometry, as of other disciplines, will depend on the type and the structure of the particular problem which it is intended to solve.

It seems clear from the foregoing that the attitude in methodology of perceiving data as quantities refers equally to a "special case" in the development of economic reality and economic thought, implying that other "cases" are possible if the type of economic structure and the related thought has changed.[20] At the same time, it must be kept in mind that it is maintained that the quantitative approach to economic problems was correct at that time; but it is stressed here that the correctness of the method (*a*) existed *in effect*, and not by virtue of any extraneous logic or eternal verity of the method, and (*b*) depended upon the ability of the economic society to continue to expand for the time being and thus to alleviate and for all practical purposes to make invisible the already actually developing structural changes within that society. When, however, these changes began to exceed the existing potentialities of expansion, the quantitative concepts began to show their inadequacy, even with regard to "overt" phenomena, and their application inevitably produced results which were wrong in proportion to the increase in the margin of error between ideally conceived economic mechanics and actually existing economic dynamics.

19 Riemann, *Über die Hypothesen, welche der Geometrie zugrunde liegen.* See also Niebyl, "Modern Mathematics and Some Problems of Quantity, Quality and Motion in Economic Analysis," *Journal of the Philosophy of Science,* VII, Part 1, (January, 1940), pp. 103 ff.
20 Keynes, *The General Theory of Employment, Interest, and Money,* especially the Introduction.

10 · Some Conclusions on the Classical Quantity Theory of Money

IT is the purpose of our exposition to retrace the process by which classical economic theory and with it an equilibristic theory of money came into existence at an early stage of industrial society. We found that economic theory, as indeed every theory that attempts to make intelligible the problems confronting society at a given time, has to be recognized as a part of that specific economic setting from which it has evolved. Money was treated as a particular problem as long as industrial production itself was only one of the ways by which people lived at that time. To the extent to which industrial production came to predominate as a way of social existence, its particular functional constituents, such as money, were perceived in a larger setting and no longer as phenomena directly and by themselves observable and describable as such. At the same time when there originated this thinking in terms of systems and the perception of specific economic phenomena as parts of these systems, society gained momentum, and theory, which existed as an expression of the economic problems of the preceding period, was just left behind, instead of being adapted and redirected to the newly developed circumstances of which it was supposedly giving testimony.

It is at this stage in the economic development and its related thought that money, previously considered the medium for the accomplishment of concrete transactions, is made to assume independence of a higher order and in this independence to symbolize the methodological attitude of the industrial leaders and the social groups related to them. The elusive and phenomenological character of money lent itself, as did no other existing concept, to the description of the mechanism of the accepted static systematics of production and distribution. The continuation of the process of production to still higher forms of division of labor, the existence of absentee ownership as the typical form of industrial enterprise (that is, the gradual emergence of growing groups living from incomes, though they themselves were separated from active participation in production) and the continuing increase in the number of wage earners and salaried employees, whose interest in the products of their labor was forcibly restricted to the incomes they received, tended to create an attitude toward productive activity in which, because of the thoroughgoing separation between man and his products, the latter appeared in a quasi-objective form, seemingly following laws which were independent of human actions, just as the long-run mechanism of the flow of money was represented as independent of interferences by government or the directors of the Bank of England. Production appeared now to the theorists only in abstract monetary terms. In their opinion investment took the form of money holdings, additional money accruing in the form of dividend or interest income. These profits seemed equally objective to the entrepreneur, and only in the form of percentages of money-capital and compared with the monetary results of various years or of other enterprises did they enter the minds of their "producers." The consumer interest of large parts of the wage-earning and salaried groups was obviously monetary, and the importance of the commodities on the market to all the population lay in their prices.

Thus, society had reached a stage in which monetary terminology became universal, a development which was coincident with the final achievement of a picture of the process of production, in which the latter overtly tended constantly toward a total equilibrium.

It was at this moment that the modern theory of price was born, in the form of a crude marginal-utility theory. This view point expressed to perfection the prevailing attitude toward the process of production. No fundamental problems indicative of any basic qualitative changes were observable; therefore it was conveniently thought that the mechanism could and should be left alone to work itself out according to the prescribed equilibrium principles. Vital interest was displayed only in the attempt to maximize income, admirably expressed in the picture of the "economic man," whose indigenous competitive psychology had only changed its place from the sphere of production to the sphere of distribution and was now fully preoccupied with "higgling" in the market.

The fundamental lesson to be learned, therefore, from an analysis of the early phase of industrial society and its attendant thought formation, particularly the formulation of quantitative monetary concepts, is that the contemporary neglect of the dynamic character of the productive process was integral to the development of that process itself. To the degree, however, that this special condition—John Maynard Keynes's "special case"—has changed and the underlying dynamics have made themselves felt and have become apparent in the form of economic crises and finally of stagnation, which increasingly have tended to destroy the previously assumed harmony of the equilibrists, any theory of money which justly can make claim to the name will have to take into account the existing discrepancy between economic thought in the form of pure theory and economic reality.

We may express the same trend of thought in this form: the margin of error between economic analysis and economic reality could justly be neglected so long as its continuous recurrence was again and again absorbed by the expansion of industrial production. But when the mechanics of organic expansion were changing into the dynamics of economic contraction, the material basis for neglecting the margin of error disappeared and the reconstruction of economic thought became mandatory, as Adam Smith and his predecessors had been compelled to reformulate economic thought after the economic basis of mercantilism had ceased to be representative of their contemporary society.

No self-sustaining theory of money can actually be formulated. The monetary relations at any given time and the function ascribed to them can be perceived only as a reflection of ever-changing economic reality. Only analysis of the latter and the understanding of its processually changing character can give us today the clue to the meaning of money. A theory of money must, therefore, be an aspect of general economic theory, the latter being itself, or being an aspect of, a dynamic theory of social organization.

An understanding of the function of money must account for the actual status of the relations of the productive forces as well as for the functional part which its reviewers play in the given economy. The function of some reviewers, or "theorists," as representatives of some particular social groups may be such as to compel them by circumstance to exhibit a definite lag, or "margin of error," in their expositions. This error, however, as we have tried to show, can be traced; and only when we are able to account for it and thus are in the position to realign our analysis with the actual functioning of the economic forces, shall we be in a position to understand the classical theories of money.

Bibliography

Acres, W. Marston, The Bank of England from Within, 1694–1900. London, Oxford University Press, 1931.

Acworth, A. W., Financial Reconstruction in England, 1815–1822. London, King, 1925.

American Economic Association, Publications. New York, American Economic Association, 1895. Vol. X.

Andreades, A., "The Finance of Tyrant Governments in Ancient Greece," in Economic History (a supplement to the *Economic Journal*), II, (Jan. 1930), 1–18, London, Macmillan, 1933.

—— History of the Bank of England 1640 to 1903. London, King, 1924.

Angell, James W., The Behavior of Money. New York and London, McGraw-Hill, 1936.

—— "The Behavior of Money: Exploratory Studies," reviewed by Howard S. Ellis, *The Journal of Political Economy*, XLIV (October, 1936), 693–696.

—— The Recovery of Germany. London, Oxford University Press, 1929.

—— The Theory of International Prices. Cambridge, Harvard University Press, 1926.

Appeal to the People of England, the Public Companies and Monied Interests on the Renewal of the Charter of the Bank, An. London, 1742.

Ashley, Sir William J., The Economic Organization of England, an Outline History. London, Longmans, Green, 1923.

—— English Economic History and Theory. 3d ed. London, Longmans, Green, 1894.

Atkinson, Jasper, Considerations on the Propriety of the Bank of England Resuming Its Payments in Specie. London, Hatchard, 1802.

Attwood, Mathias, A Letter to Lord Archibald Hamilton on Alterations in the Value of Money. London, Ridgway, 1823.

Attwood, Thomas, A Letter to Nicholas Vansittart on the Creation of Money and on Its Action upon the National Prosperity. Birmingham, Wrightson, 1817.

—— Observations on Currency, Population, and Pauperism, in

Two Letters to Arthur Young. Birmingham, Wrightson, 1818.

—— Prosperity Restored, or Reflections on the Cause of the Public Distresses and on the Only Means of Relieving Them. London, Baldwin, Cradock & Joy, and Longman Hurst, 1817.

—— The Scotch Banker. London, Ridgway, 1832.

Bacon, Francis, Works of . . . collected and ed. by Spedding, Ellis, and Heath, Vol. I. Boston, Brown and Taggard, 1861.

Bagehot, Walter, Lombard Street; a Description of the Money Market. London, Murray, 1927.

Bank of England's Vade Mecum, The; or, Sure Guide . . . in which every office, place, and the manner of procuring notes of every sort for cash is distinctly described, by a Gentleman of the Bank. London, Becket, 1782.

Bank, the Stock Exchange, the Banker's Clearing House, the Minister and the Public, The. London, Wilson, 1821.

Barnes, Donald Grove, A History of the English Corn Laws from 1660–1846. London, Routledge, 1930.

Bentham, Jeremy, Defence of Usury. New York, Foster, 1837.

—— Works. Vols. III, X, ed. by John Bowring. Edinburgh, Tait, 1843.

Birnie, Arthur, An Economic History of the British Isles. 2d ed. London, Methuen, 1938.

—— "The Growth of Industry in Europe from the Later Middle Ages to the Present Day," European Civilization, Its Origin and Development, ed. by Edward Eyre. London, Oxford University Press, 1937.

Bloomfield, Arthur I., "Foreign-Trade Doctrines of the Physiocrats," The American Economic Review, XXVIII (December, 1938), 716–735.

Boase, Henry, A Letter to the Right Hon. Lord King in Defense of the Conduct of the Directors of the Bank of England and Ireland. . . . London, Nicol, 1804.

Bollmann, Eric, A Second Letter . . . on the Practicability of the New System of Bullion Payments. London, Murray, 1819.

Bonar, James, Malthus and His Work. New York, Macmillan, 1924.

Bosanquet, Charles, Practical Observations on the Report of the Bullion Committee. London, Richardson, 1810.

Bourne, H. R. Fox, English Merchants: Memoirs in Illustration of the Progress of British Commerce. London, Bentley, 1866.

Boyd, Walter, A Letter to the Right Honourable William Pitt on the Influence of the Stoppage of Issues in Specie at the Bank of England. London, Wright, 1801.

British Parliamentary Papers, see Great Britain, Parliament.

Bucher, Carl, Industrial Evolution; trans. from the 3d German ed. by S. Horley Wickett. New York, Holt, 1904.

Burgess, Henry, A Letter to the Right Honorable George Canning. . . . London, Harvey and Darton; Ridgway, 1826.

Burnes, Arthur Robert, The Decline of Competition; a Study of the Evolution of American Industry. New York and London, McGraw-Hill, 1938.

Cairnes, J. E., Essays in Political Economy, Theoretical and Applied. London, Macmillan, 1873.

Cannan, Edwin, Modern Currency and the Regulation of Its Value. London, King, 1931.

—— Money, 5th ed. Westminster, King, 1926.

Cassel, Gustav, The Crisis in the World's Monetary System. Oxford, Clarendon Press, 1932.

—— Post-War Monetary Stabilization. New York, Columbia University Press, 1928.

—— The Theory of Social Economy, trans. by Joseph McCabe. London, Unwin, n.d.

Clapham, J. H., The Economic Development of France and Germany, 1815–1914. Cambridge, The University Press, 1921.

—— An Economic History of Modern Britain; Vol. I: The Early Railway Age, 1820–1850; Vol. II: Free Trade and Steel, 1850–1886; Vol. III: Machines and National Rivalries, 1887–1914, with an Epilogue, 1914–1929. Cambridge, The University Press, 1926–1938.

Cobbett, J. M., and J. P. Cobbett, *Weekly Political Register,* October 20, 1821, pp. 925 ff. London, A. Cobbett, 1835.

Committee of Secrecy, *see* Great Britain, Parliament.

Cournot, August, Researches into the Mathematical Principles of the Theory of Wealth, trans. by N. T. Bacon. New York, Macmillan, 1897.

Cunningham, Wm., An Essay on Western Civilization in Its Economic Aspects. Cambridge, The University Press, 1902.

—— The Growth of English Industry and Commerce. Cambridge, The University Press, 1912.

—— Modern Civilization, in Some of Its Economic Aspects. London, Methuen, 1896.

Dempsey, Bernard W., "The Historical Emergence of Quantity Theory," *Quarterly Journal of Economics,* L (November, 1935), 174–184.

Dickinson, Henry Winram, John Wilkinson, Iron Master, 1914.

Dictionary of Political Economy, ed. by Sir Robert Harry Inglis Palgrave. London, Macmillan, 1915.

Dobb, Maurice, Political Economy and Capitalism. London, Rout-ledge, 1937.

Easton, H. T., Money Exchange and Banking in Their Practical, Theoretical and Legal Aspects, 2d ed. London, Pitman, 1907.

Ehrenberg, Richard, Capital and Finance in the Age of the Renaissance. New York, Harcourt, Brace, n.d.

English Economic History, Select Documents; comp. and ed. by A. E. Bland, P. A. Brown, R. H. Tawney. 2d ed. London, Bell, 1915.

Escher, Franklin, Foreign Exchange Explained. New York, Macmillan, 1930.

Famous Utopias; Introd. by Charles M. Andrews (texts of Rousseau, More, Bacon, and Campanella). New York, Tudor [1937].

Feaveryear, A. E., "Banking and Finance in Europe and the United States, 1793–1933," in European Civilization, Its Origin and Development, Vol. V, ed. by Edward Eyre. London, Oxford University Press, 1937.

—— "General Introduction to the Modern Period," in European Civilization, Its Origin and Development, Vol. V, ed. by Edward Eyre. London, Oxford University Press, 1937.

—— The Pound Sterling. London, Oxford University Press, 1932.

Fisher, Irving, The Theory of Interest. New York, Macmillan, 1930.

Förster, Walter, Theorie der Währungsentwertung. Berlin, Fischer, 1936.

Fong, H. D., Triumph of the Factory System in England. Tientsin, China, Chihli Press, 1930.

Fraser, L. M., Economic Thought and Language: a Critique of Some Fundamental Economic Concepts. London, Black, 1937.

Fullerton, John, On the Regulation of Currency, 2d ed., 1845.

Garis, Roy L., Principles of Money, Credit and Banking. New York, Macmillan, 1934.

Gaskell, Phillip, Artisans and Machinery. London, Parker, 1836.

Gide, Charles, and Charles Rist, Geschichte der Volkswirtschaftlichen Lehrmeinungen. Jena, Fischer, 1923.

Giffen, Sir R., The Growth of Capital. London, Bell, 1889.

Godfrey, Michael, A Brief Account of the Intended Bank of England. London, Taylor, 1694.

Gossen, Hermann Heinrich, Entwickelung der Gesetze des menschlichen Verkehrs. Berlin, Prager, 1889.

Great Britain, Parliament, Report of "Select Committee of the Restrictions Imposed and the Privileges Conferred by Law on Bankers Authorized to Make and Issue Notes in England, Scotland and Ireland Respectively." 1775 (351), IX,

—— Reports of House of Commons "Committee of Secrecy on the Outstanding Demands of the Bank of England; and Restrictions on Payments in Cash by the Minute of the Council." 1797 (18–26), XI.

—— Report of the "Select Committee on the High Price of Bullion." 1813 (349), III.

—— Report by the House of Lords "Secret Committee to Inquire into the State of the Bank of England; with Reference to the Expediency of the Resumption of Cash Payments." 1819 (291), III; 1819 (202), III; 1819 (282), III.

—— Report of "Secret Committee on Joint Stock Banks on the Operation of Act 7 Geo. IV c. 46, Permitting the Establishment of Joint Stock Banks." 1836 (591), IX.

Gregory, T. E., Select Statutes, Documents and Reports Relating to British Banking, 1832–1928, Introduction by Gregory. London, Oxford University Press, 1929.

—— The Westminster Bank through a Century. London, Oxford University Press, 1936.

Grindon, L. H., Manchester Banks and Bankers: Historical Biographical and Anecdotal. Manchester, Palmer and Howe, 1878.

Haberler, Gottfried von, Der Sinn der Indexzahlen. Tübingen, Mohr (Paul Siebeck), 1927.

—— The Theory of International Trade. New York, Macmillan, 1937.

Hall, Walter, A View of Our Late and of Our Future Currency. London, 1819.

Hammond, J. L., and Barbara Hammond, The Rise of Modern Industry. New York, Harcourt, Brace, 1937.

Hansard, T. C., Parliamentary Debates, XIII, XL. London, 1825.

Hawtrey, R. G., The Art of Central Banking. London, Longmans, Green, 1933.

—— "British Banking and Finance 1793–1931," in European Civilization, Its Origin and Development, Vol. V, ed. by Edward Eyre. London, Oxford University Press, 1937.

—— Currency and Credit. 2d ed. London, Longmans, Green, 1923.

Hayek, F. A. von, Monetary Theory and the Trade Cycle; trans. by N. Kaldor and H. M. Croome. New York, Harcourt, Brace (1933).

—— "The Mythology of Capital," Quarterly Journal of Economics, L (Feb., 1936), 199–228.

—— "A Note on the Development of the Doctrine of 'Forced Savings,'" Quarterly Journal of Economics, XLVII (Nov., 1932), 123–133.

—— Prices and Production. London, Routledge, 1931.

Heaton, Herbert, Economic History of Europe. New York and London, Harper, 1936.

Heckscher, Eli F., Mercantilism; authorized trans. by Mendel Shapiro. Vols. I–II. London, Allen & Unwin, 1935.

Hill, John, An Inquiry into the Causes of the Present High Price of Gold Bullion. London, Longman, Hurst, Rees, Orme and Brown, 1810.

Hobbes, Thomas, Leviathan. London, Routledge, 1887.

Hobson, John A., The Evolution of Modern Capitalism; a Study of Machine Production. London, Scott; New York, Scribner, 1907.

—— Incentives in the New Industrial Order. London, Parsons, 1922.

Hodges, James, The Present State of England as to Coin and Publick Charges. London, Bell, 1697.

Hogben, Lancelot, Political Arithmetic. London, Allen and Unwin, 1938.

Hollander, J. H., "The Development of the Theory of Money from Adam Smith to David Ricardo," The Quarterly Journal of Economics, XXV (May, 1911), 429–470.

Holtrop, M. W., "Theories of the Velocity of Circulation of Money in Earlier Economic Literature," in Economic History (a supplement to the Economic Journal), I (Jan., 1929), 503–534, London, Macmillan, 1929.

Huberman, Leo, Man's Worldly Goods. New York, Harper, 1936.

Hughes, John (of Liverpool), Liverpool Banks and Bankers 1760–1837; a History of the Circumstances Which Gave Rise to the Industry and of the Men Who Founded and Developed It. Liverpool, Young, 1906.

Hume, David, Essays, Moral, Political and Literary; ed. by T. H. Green and T. H. Grose. London, Longmans, Green, 1875.

Huskisson, W., The Question concerning the Depreciation of Our Currency Stated. London, Murray, 1810.

Hutchison, T. W., The Significance and Basic Postulates of Economic Theory. London, Macmillan, 1938.

James, Henry, Essays on Money, Exchanges and Political Economy. London, Hunter and Manchee, 1820.

Jevons, W. Stanley, The Coal Question. London and Cambridge, Macmillan, 1865.

—— Investigations in Currency & Finance. 2d ed. London, Macmillan, 1909.

—— Money and the Mechanism of Exchange. New York, Appleton, 1876.

Johnson, E. A. J., Predecessors of Adam Smith, the Growth of British Economic Thought. New York, Prentice-Hall, 1937.

Joplin, Thomas, An Analysis and History of the Currency Question together with an Account of the Origin and Growth of Joint-Stock Banking in England. London, Ridgway, 1832.

—— An Essay on the General Principles and Present Practice of Banking in England and Scotland. . . . London, Baldwin, Cradock and Joy, 1822.

—— An Examination of the Report of the Joint-Stock Bank Committee, etc., etc. 3d ed. London, Ridgway, 1837.

—— Views on the Corn Bill of 1827, and Other Measures of Government. London, Ridgway and Baldwin, Cradock and Joy, 1828.

—— Views on the Currency in Which the Connexion between Corn and Currency Is Shown: the Nature of Our System of Currency Explained. . . . , London, Ridgway, 1828.

Judges, A. V., "Money, Finance and Banking from the Renaissance to the Eighteenth Century," in European Civilization, Its Origin and Development, Vol. V, ed. by Edward Eyre. London, Oxford University Press, 1937.

Keynes, John Maynard, The General Theory of Employment, Interest and Money. London, Macmillan, 1936.

King, Frank H., "The Ricardian Theory of Production and Distribution," The Canadian Journal of Economics and Political Science, I (February, 1935).

King, W. T. C., History of the London Discount Market. London, Routledge, 1936.

Knight, Melvin M., Economic History of Europe, to the End of the Middle Ages. Boston, New York, Houghton Mifflin, 1926.

Latimer, Hugh, Seven Sermons before Edward VI, 1549, in English Reprints. Vol. VI, ed. by Edward Arber.

Lauderdale, J. M., An Inquiry into the Nature and Origin of Public Wealth and into the Means and Causes of Its Increase. 2d ed. London, Longmans, Hurst, and Hurst, Robinson and Co., 1818.

—— The Lauderdale Papers; ed. by Osmund Airy. Vol. I, 1639–1667; Vol. II, 1667–1673; Vol. III, 1673–1679. Westminster, Nichols, 1884, 1885.

Lexis, W., Erörterungen über die Währungsfrage. Leipzig, Duncker and Humblot, 1881.

Lipson, E., The Economic History of England. Vol. I, The Middle Ages. London, Adam and Charles Black, 1937.

Locke, John, The Works. . . . London, J. Churchill and S. Manship, 1714.

Loewe, Adolf, Economics and Sociology; a Plea for Cooperation in the Social Sciences. London, Allen & Unwin, 1935.

Lord, John, Capital and Steam-Power, 1750–1800. London, King, 1923.

"Lord King's Thoughts on the Restriction of Payments in Specie at the Banks of England and Ireland," *Edinburgh Review*, IV (July, 1803), 402–421 (bound Vol. No. II).

Lundberg, Erik, Studies in the Theory of Economic Expansion. London, King [1937]. Stockholm Economic Studies.

McCulloch, John Ramsay, Historical Sketch of the Bank of England. London, Manning, 1831.

—— Old and Scarce Tracts of Money. London, King, 1933.

[Malthus, T. R.], "Depreciation of Paper Currency" [a review of pamphlets by Charles Bosanquet and David Ricardo], *Edinburgh Review*, XVII (February, 1811), 340–372. Bound Vol. XVII.

Malthus, T. R., An Essay on the Principle of Population, 1798–1803. Vols. I, II. New York, Macmillan; London, Macmillan, 1909.

—— Observations on the Effects of the Corn Laws, 1814. Baltimore, The Johns Hopkins Press, 1932.

—— On the Principle of Population. Vol. I. London, Dent; New York, Dutton, 1927. Everyman's Library.

—— The Principles of Political Economy, 2d ed.; reprinted by the London School of Economics and Political Science, London, 1936.

Marget, Arthur W., "Léon Walrus and the 'Cash-Balance Approach' to the Problem of the Value of Money," *Journal of Political Economy*, XXXIX (October, 1931), 569–600.

—— The Theory of Prices: a Re-examination of the Central Problems of Monetary Theory. New York, Prentice-Hall, 1938.

Marshall, Alfred, Industry and Trade. London, Macmillan, 1919.

—— Official Papers. London, Macmillan, 1926.

—— Principles of Economics, 8th ed. London, Macmillan, 1920.

—— The Pure Theory of Foreign Trade, The Pure Theory of Domestic Values; reprinted by the London School of Economics and Political Science. London, 1930.

Marx, Karl, A Contribution to the Critique of Political Economy. Chicago, Kerr, 1911.

Matthews, Philip W., The Bankers' Clearing House. London, Pitman, 1921.

Menger, Dr. Anton, Das Recht auf den vollen Arbeitsertrag. Stuttgart, Cotta, 1891.

Meteyard, E., The Life of Josiah Wedgwood from His Private

Correspondence and Family Papers. London, Hurst and Blacket, 1865–1866.

Mill, John Stuart, Principles of Political Economy, ed. by W. J. Ashley. London, Longmans, Green, 1926.

—— "Review of William Blake's Observations on the Effects Produced by the Expenditure of Government," *Westminster Review,* Vol. I (1824).

Mises, Ludwig von, The Theory of Money and Credit; trans. by H. E. Batson. New York, Harcourt Brace, 1936.

Mnoilesco, Mihail, The Theory of Protection and International Trade. London, King, 1931.

Monroe, Arthur Eli, Early Economic Thought. Cambridge, Harvard University Press, 1924.

More, Sir Thomas, Utopia, 1516; in English Reprints, Vol. VI, ed. by Edward Arber. Birmingham, 1669.

Morton, A. L., A People's History of England. London, Gollancz, 1938.

Muirhead, James P., Life of James Watt. London, Murray, 1858.

Mun, Thomas, A Discourse of Trade from England unto the East Indies Answering to Diverse Objections Which Are Usually Made against the Same. London, Pyper, 1621.

—— England's Treasure by Forraign Trade, or, The Balance of Our Forraign Trade Is the Rule of Our Treasure. Ashley ed. 1664.

Newbold, J. T. Walton, Democracy, Debts and Disarmament. New York, Dutton, 1933.

Niebyl, K. H., "Historijske Izmjene u Funkciji Izvoza Kapitala," *Ekonomist* (Zagreb), Nos. 7–8 (July–August, 1939), 284–292.

—— "The Need for a Concept of Value in Economic Theory," *Quarterly Journal of Economics,* LIV (February, 1940), 201–216.

—— "Modern Mathematics and Some Problems of Quantity, Quality and Motion in Economic Analysis," *Journal of the Philosophy of Science,* VII, No. 1 (Jan., 1940), 103–120.

Oncken, August, Geschichte der Nationalökonomie. Leipzig, Hirschfeld, 1902.

Overstone, Lord S. J. L., Tracts and Other Publications on Metallic and Paper Currency. London, Harrison, 1857.

Paliner, A. N., John Wilkinson and the Old Bersham Iron Works. 1899.

Palmer, John Horsely, Evidence in the Report from the Commons Committee of Secrecy on the Bank of England Charter. 1832.

—— Reply to the Reflections, etc., of Mr. Samuel Jones Loyd. London, Richardson, 1837.

Parnell, Sir Henry, Observations on Paper Money, Banking and Overtrading.

Pennington, James, A Letter to Kirkman Finlay, Esq., on the Importation of Foreign Corn and the Value of the Precious Metals in Different Countries. London, Simpkin, Marshall, 1840.

Petty, Sir Wm., The Political Anatomy of Ireland, 1691, in *Economic Writings*, Cambridge, The University Press, 1899.

—— *Politicall Arithmetick.*

—— *Quantulumque.* 1862.

Phillips, Maberly, A History of Banks, Bankers and Banking in Northumberland, Durham and North Yorkshire. London, Effingham, Wilson, 1894.

Prentice, David, Thoughts on the Repeal of the Bank Restriction Law. London, Murray, 1811.

Rae, George, The Country Banker, His Clients, Cares, and Work. New York, Scribner's, 1920.

Rau, K. H., Lehrbuch der politischen Ökonomie. 4th ed. Leipzig and Heidelberg, Winter, 1850–1869.

Reprint of Economic Tracts, A, ed. by Jacob H. Hollander. Baltimore, The Johns Hopkins Press, 1906.

Ricardo, David, "High Price of Bullion," from The Works of David Ricardo, ed. by J. R. McCulloch. London, Murray, 1846.

—— Letters of . . . to Hutches Trower, and Others; ed. by James Bonar and J. H. Hollander. Oxford, Clarendon Press, 1899.

—— Letters of . . . to Thomas Robert Malthus, 1810–1823; ed. by James Bonar. London, Clarendon Press, 1887.

—— Letters to John Ramsay McCulloch, 1816–1823; ed. by J. H. Hollander. New York, Macmillan, 1895.

—— Minor Papers on the Currency Question, 1809–1823; ed. by J. H. Hollander. Baltimore, The Johns Hopkins Press, 1932.

—— Notes on Malthus' Principles of Political Economy; ed. by J. H. Hollander and T. E. Gregory. Baltimore, The Johns Hopkins Press, 1926.

—— Principles of Political Economy and Taxation; ed. by E. C. K. Connor. London, Bell, 1891.

—— *The Works of* . . . London, Murray, 1846.

Richards, R. D., The Early History of Banking in England. London, King, 1929.

Riemann, Uber die Hypothesen, welche der Geometrie zugrunde liegen. Göttingen, 1854: Sonderausgabe mit Erläuterungen von Weyl, 1923.

Robbins, Lionel, An Essay on the Nature and Significance of Economic Science. 2d ed. London, Macmillan, 1937.

Roll, Erich, An Early Experiment in Industrial Organization, Be-
ing a History of the Firm of Boulton & Watt, 1775–1805. Lon-
don, New York, Toronto, Longmans, Green, 1930.
—— A History of Economic Thought. London, Faber and Faber,
1938.
Rooke, John, An Inquiry into the Principles of National Wealth.
Edinburgh, Balfour, 1824.
—— Remarks on the Nature and Operation of Money, 1819.
Rose, George, A Brief Examination into the Increase of the Reve-
nue, Commerce and Navigation of Great Britain, from 1792–
1799. 4th ed. London, Hatchard, 1799.
Rosse, Lawrence Parsons, 2d Earl of, Observations on the Present
State of the Currency of England. London, Stockdale, 1811.
Salzman, L. F., English Industries of the Middle Ages. Oxford,
Clarendon Press, 1923.
Say, Jean-Baptiste, Letters to Malthus on Political Economy and
Stagnation of Commerce. London, Harding's Bookshop, 1936.
—— A Treatise on Political Economy or the Production, Distribu-
tion and Consumption of Wealth; trans., from the 4th French
ed. by C. R. Prinsep. Philadelphia, Grigg, 1830.
Schumpeter, Joseph A., Business Cycles. New York, McGraw-Hill,
1939.
—— The Theory of Economic Development. Cambridge, Harvard
University Press, 1934.
Scott, W. R., The Constitution and Finance of English, Scottish
and Irish Joint-Stock Companies to 1720. Cambridge, The Uni-
versity Press, 1912.
Senior, Nassau William, Letters on the Factory Act as It Affects
the Cotton Manufacture. London, Fellowes, 1837.
—— An Outline of the Science of Political Economy. New York,
Farrar and Rinehart, 1939.
—— Three Lectures on the Transmission of the Precious Metals
from Country to Country, and the Mercantile Theory of Wealth.
2d ed. London, Murray, 1830.
Shannon, H. A., "The Coming of General Limited Liability," in
Economic History (a supplement to the Economic Journal), II
(Jan., 1931), 267–291, London, Macmillan, 1933.
—— "The First Five Thousand Limited Companies and Their
Duration," in Economic History (a supplement to the Economic
Journal), II (Jan., 1932), 396–424, London, Macmillan, 1933.
Silberling, Norman J., "British Prices and Business Cycles," Re-
view of Economic Statistics, Preliminary Vol. V, Supplement
No. 2 (October, 1923), 219–262.
—— "Financial and Monetary Policy of Great Britain during the

Napoleonic Wars," I: Financial Policy (Feb., 1924), 214–233; II: Ricardo and the Bullion Report (May, 1924), 397–440; *Quarterly Journal of Economics*, Vol. XXXVIII.

Simmel, Georg, Philosophie des Geldes. Leipzig, Duncker & Humblot, 1900.

Smith, Adam, Wealth of Nations; 2d ed., ed. by Edwin Cannan. London, Methuen, 1920.

Sombart, W., Der Moderne Kapitalismus. 4th ed. München and Leipzig, Duncker & Humblot, 1921.

Stewart, Dugald, The Collected Works of; ed. by Sir William Hamilton. Edinburgh, Constable, 1855.

Swingler, Stephen, An Outline of Political Thought since the French Revolution. London, Gollancz, 1939.

Tawney, R. H., Religion and the Rise of Capitalism; a Historical Study. New York, Harcourt, Brace, 1936.

Tawney, R. H., and E. Power, "Memorandum on the Reasons Moving Queen Elizabeth to Reform the Coinage, 1559," Tudor Economic Documents. London, New York, Longmans, Green, 1924.

Thomas, S. E., Rise and Growth of Joint Stock Banking. London, Pitman, 1934.

Thompson, T. P., "On the Instrument of Exchange," *Westminster Review*, I (1824).

Thornton, Henry, An Enquiry into the Nature and Effects of the Paper Credit of Great Britain. London, Hatchard, 1802.

Tooke, Thomas, and William Newmarch, A History of Prices and of the State of the Circulation from 1792 to 1856. London, King, 1928.

Torrens, Robert, A Comparative Estimate of the Effects Which a Continuance and a Removal of the Restriction upon Cash Payments Are Respectively Calculated to Produce: with Strictures on Mr. Ricardo's Proposal for Obtaining a Secure and Economical Currency. London, R. Hunter, 1819.

—— An Essay on Money and Paper Currency. London, Johnson, 1812.

—— A Letter to the Right Honourable Viscount Melbourne, on the Causes of the Recent Derangement in the Money Market and on Bank Reform. London, Longmans, Reese, Orme, Brown and Green, 1827.

Trawter, Coutts, The Principle of Currency and Exchange. 1810.

Turner, Samuel, Considerations upon the Agriculture Commerce and Manufacture of the British Empire. London, Murray, 1822.

—— A Letter Addressed to the Right Hon. Robert Peel.

Ure, Andrew, Philosophy of Manufactures (continued in its details to the present time by P. L. Simmonds). 3d ed. London, Bohn, 1861.

Usher, Abbott Payson, An Introduction to the Industrial History of England. Cambridge, Houghton Mifflin, 1919.

Veblen, Thorstein, The Theory of Business Enterprise. New York, Scribners, 1920.

—— The Theory of the Leisure Class. New York, Macmillan, 1899.

Verax (*i.e.*, Richard Groom), The Bank of England Defended, or the Principal Cause of High Prices Demonstrated.

Viner, Jacob, Studies in the Theory of International Trade. New York, Harper, 1937.

Walker, Francis A., International Bimetallism. New York, Holt, 1896.

Weber, Max, General Economic History. New York, Greenberg, 1927.

—— The Protestant Ethic and the Spirit of Capitalism. London, Allen and Unwin, 1930.

Wheatley, John, Remarks on Currency and Commerce. London, Cadell and Davies, 1803.

Wilson, James, Capital, Currency, and Banking. 2d ed. London, Aird, 1859.

Wilson, Thomas, A Discourse upon Usury. New York, Harcourt, Brace, no date. Historical Introduction by R. H. Tawney.

Woods, George, Observations on the Present Price of Bullion and Rates of Exchange. London, Baldwin, 1811.

Yonge, Charles Duke, The Life of Lord Liverpool. London, Macmillan, 1868.

Index